BEHAVIORAL MEDICINE MADE RIDICULOUSLY SIMPLE

by

Frank C. Seitz, Ph.D., ABPP
Private Practice
Adjunct Professor of Medical Science
Montana State University
University of Washington School of Medicine

MedMaster, Inc., Miami

ISBN 0-940780-29-1

Made in the United States of America

Published by
MedMaster, Inc.
P.O. Box 640028
Miami, FL 33164

DEDICATION

To my colleagues, patients, and
family!

ACKNOWLEDGMENTS

Although my name is used as the single author of this book, in fact a number of authors were "sitting on my shoulder, whispering in my ears, and guiding my pen" as this work evolved and took shape. For that reason, I prefer to use the pronoun "we" and "our," rather than "I" or "mine," in sharing *our* thoughts and insights about behavioral medicine. We wish to recognize the WAMI (Washington, Alaska, Montana and Idaho Regional Medical School Program) and University of Washington School of Medicine faculty and students who have participated in the System of Human Behavior class over the past 25 years.

Our gratitude is extended to the following Course Chairmen for their knowledge, writing, and wisdom, which are sprinkled generously throughout this book:

John E. Carr, Ph.D., Mark Covey, Ph.D., Hal Dengerink, Ph.D., Robert Gregory, Ph.D., Bruno Kappes, Ph.D., Phil Mohan, Ph.D., and Ed Walker, M.D.

Our deep appreciation is given to the following lecturers, authors, mentors, supporters, and contributors who have provided material upon which this book is based:

Douglas Alvord, M.D.
Albert S. Carlin, Ph.D.
John E. Carr, Ph.D.
Mark Covey, Ph.D.
William Dement, M.D.
David Elkind, Ph.D.
Dr. Erik Erickson
Barbara Fadem, Ph.D.

William Fordyce, Ph.D.
Sigmund Freud, M.D.
Dr. Jack Gordan
Gary Gullickson
Dr. Steven Guggenheim
Dan Hunt, M.D.
Roger Katz, Ph.D.
Wayne Katon, M.D.

Dr. Elizabeth Kubler-Ross
Dr. Hank Levine
John Loeser, M.D.
Frank Newman, Ph.D.
Dr. Jean Piaget
William Prunty, M.D.
Victor Raimy, Ph.D.
Dr. Gretchen Schodde

Mark Schuckit, M.D.   Michael Simpson, M.D.   William Womack, M.D.
Roy Schwarz, M.D.   Alan Stoudemire, M.D.   Steven Zlutnik, Ph.D.
Hans Selye, M.D., Ph.D.   Paul Visscher, M.D.
Frederick Sierles, M.D.   Danny Wedding, Ph.D.

The Overlooked Contributor (Our apologies!)

Special thanks to Laura Seitz for her editing and to Adele Seitz for her proofreading and cover design—and for their ongoing encouragement when we were tempted to "give it up."

Although his name has been mentioned twice in these acknowledgments, my dear friend, superb editor, and treasured colleague, Jack Carr, has to be given yet another "curtain call." Jack has been a guiding light for the behavioral sciences and behavioral medicine for years, and continues (fortunately for all of us) to provide a depth of scholarship, commitment, and common sense so badly needed within the mental health community.

A final thanks to Stephen Goldberg, M.D., of MedMaster, Inc., who had the confidence in our book to publish it, and who understands that behavioral medicine is anything but ridiculously simple.

Frank C. Seitz, Ph.D.
and Friends

FOREWORD

Generations of medical students have struggled to comprehend the complex and seemingly esoteric language of the social and behavioral sciences and to understand their relevance to the practice of medicine. The emergence of the Biopsychosocial Model as the preeminent approach to medical practice underscores the increasingly important role that Behavioral Medicine plays in modern medical education and health care. With progressive recognition comes increasing familiarity with terms and concepts as medical educators discover new ways to demonstrate both the pragmatism and relevance of Behavioral Medicine.

Dr. Frank Seitz, a clinical psychologist, has taught Behavioral Medicine to beginning medical students in the regional medical program (Washington, Alaska, Montana, Idaho) of the University of Washington School of Medicine for 25 years. His inimitable style of teaching, which combines personal experiences as both patient and clinician, conversations with practitioners and visiting professors, lay persons, and patients, and an extraordinary capacity for explaining principles and procedures through analogy, metaphor and humor have earned him a well deserved reputation as an outstanding teacher. Sometimes unpredictable, but always challenging and informative, his presentations of Behavioral Medicine principles have been eagerly sought and imitated by colleagues. In this volume he shares them more broadly, highlighting the humor and human interest inherent in his approach and ever reminding us that behavioral science has been an integral part of the evolution of the practice of medicine since Org, the Neanderthal, first considered managed care. Tongue-in-cheek comments aside, Dr. Seitz, along with his colleagues, indeed appreciates that Behavioral Medicine is an awesome art/science that is anything but Ridiculously Simple.

John E. Carr, Ph.D., A.B.P.P.
Professor of Psychiatry & Behavioral Sciences
    and Psychology
University of Washington
Seattle, Washington, 1997

TABLE OF CONTENTS

Section III: Developmental Stages

CHAPTER 1

INTRODUCTION: TO DOCTORS WHO WANT TO BE HEALERS

She didn't want to die. In fact, she watched her blood chemistries like a hawk, hoping that their staying within normal levels would herald the remission of her ovarian cancer. She had so much to live for—her family, her friends, her horses and dogs, her love of life. As she lay bloated with fluid in her abdomen, her pleading eyes scanned her doctor: "Doctor, what is going to happen to me?" He could have given statistics. He could have reviewed her symptoms and told her what her deteriorating body already knew. Instead, he saw the fear in her look and chose to connect with her soul.

"Fay," he spoke gently, "several things might happen in the next few days." He then explained two likely complications, excessive fluid buildup and intestinal obstructions, and what he would recommend about dealing with them. But his words and manner said much more. He dared to journey into her frightened heart. He held her hand, encouraging her to voice her unspeakable fears. Her sigh of relief told him and our waiting family that she was peaceful again, taking yet another courageous step toward facing her dragons of fear and living life to its fullest. Fay had not been "cured" but she had been "healed." And her Doctor (truly a Doctor with a capital *D*) had helped in this healing.

Fay's body died three weeks later, but her spirit continued to dance with life, unfettered by fear, right up until the time she drew her final breath. Part of this dance was empowered by her physician, an excellent doctor who had also chosen to be a healer.

As a medical student you will be well prepared scientifically to battle biological disease. The contributors to this book hope to encourage you to move beyond grappling only with disease and to attempt the more demanding task of dealing with illness, both as a scientist and as a healer. Our mission is serious, but we hope occasionally to sprinkle the "facts" with some humor. To quote Oscar Wilde, "Life is too important to be taken seriously." If this observation is true of life, it impresses us as certainly true of medicine.

As you will read in subsequent chapters, "disease" does not occur in a vacuum. It is the result of a complex, constantly changing interaction of biology, environment, and behavior. Indeed, much of the suffering you will find yourself treating as a physician will have emotional, behavioral, cognitive, environmental, and socio-cultural components rather than being purely biological in nature. This book is designed to enhance your appreciation of the "behavioral system" as a point of integration among all of the organ systems. The interface between you, the physician, and your patient is behavioral. An increased understanding of human behavior will improve the quality of care you deliver to your patients. Further, as the evidence is clear that behavioral factors are important in the illness process, a better understanding of what those factors are and how they can be modified will also improve your efficiency as a practicing physician.

Section I, "Overview, Models, and Mechanisms of Intervention," will focus on the context in which medicine is practiced, introducing a **biopsychosocial model** that provides a comprehensive context in which the doctor-patient interaction can be viewed. Within the biopsychosocial model, specific **behavioral medicine strategies** will be discussed, including an overview of behavioral principles useful in medical treatment. Offering a counterpoint to a strictly behavioral approach to understanding human behavior, a **psychoanalytic** conceptualization of our patients and ourselves will be considered. Then, we will try to wax eloquently about important components of **doctor-patient communications.** Finally, the **family** and its role in patient treatment will be discussed.

Section II, "Clinical Problems," will focus on specific patient difficulties which lend themselves to behavioral intervention and analysis, including:

> stress
> chronic pain
> depression
> suicidal behavior
> alcohol abuse
> drug abuse
> sleep disorders
> domestic violence
> sexual abuse

Section III, "Developmental Stages," will deal with the phases of human growth and the behavioral medicine implications of specific illnesses and diseases in each stage:

> Infancy
> Childhood
> Adolescence
> Young Adulthood

Middle Age
Old Age
Dying and Death

In discussing disease and illness within a behavioral context and within human developmental stages, it is our hope to impress upon you the critical need to perceive your patients within a more clinically useful, yet more complex, biopsychosocial framework.

Whew! Takes your breath away, doesn't it?! Put more simply, we hope to help you view your patients within the "Big Picture," releasing you from seeing them only with respect to their body organ systems. A biomedical perspective is important, but we want to stretch your personal and professional perspective so that you will be able to heal folks like Fay, and become a doctor with a capital *D*.

SECTION I

OVERVIEW, MODELS, AND MECHANISMS OF INTERVENTION

CHAPTER 2

THE BIOPSYCHOSOCIAL MODEL OF HEALTH CARE: MORE THAN JUST A BAG OF BONES

Bet you five dollars that you wanted to skip this chapter! Why should an overworked medical student like you read behavioral science "stuff" when there's anatomy and physiology to memorize?!

Disease vs. Illness

One reason: you want to become an excellent physician . . . which means treating not only the patient's **disease** (i.e., biological pathology) but also the patient's **illness** (i.e., a person's total response to disease, including biological, psychological, and social reactions). You need to treat both to be a healer. Your patient's **behavior** is the primary clinical data from which you assess and treat your patient's condition. Since the interaction between you and your patient is behavioral, it doesn't take a rocket scientist to figure out that an increased understanding of human behavior on your part will improve the quality of care you deliver to your patients. The more you understand about human behavior, the better doctor you become.

Mortality and Behavior

Overwhelming research evidence underlines the importance of behavioral factors in the illness process. More than two decades ago, the Surgeon General of the United States released a shocking report that of the ten leading causes of death in the U.S. (heart disease, cancer, etc.), **50% of the mortality can be traced to be-havioral factors** (smoking, drinking, overeating, poor exercise habits, stress, etc.). That picture remains the same today.

Roots of the Biomedical Model: Reductionism and Dualism

Before there were CAT scans, before penicillin was discovered, before surgery was done by barbers, even before there were hospital administrators, HMOs and Medicare . . . there was behavior. In attempting to understand and explain disease and illness (i.e., pathological behavior), prehistorical primitive medicine developed a world view which assumed a close interrelationship between the human, nature, and the divine. Our bodies were not considered "biological islands" cut off from the rest of our humanity. Because little was understood of biology, the physical and spiritual were not sharply distinguished. Magic and medicine merged in the primitives' attempt to understand and control their world. Treatment rituals commonly used confession and suggestion aimed at reintegration of the disturbed individual into the existing social and spiritual structure. The focus of treatment was on illness rather than disease, albeit in a primitive fashion, as healers worked to restore harmony and balance within the patient's intrapersonal and interpersonal universe.

Although early health care practitioners like the ancient Greek physicians lacked high tech instrumentation, they made up for some scientific deficiencies with their respect and appreciation for the **meaning** of disease (i.e., how biological pathology was perceived by the patient and how it impacted perceptions of self, family, and social environment). This early biopsychosocial perspective did not generate healers with stethoscopes, but they were healers nevertheless. The medical skills and perspectives of these Greek physicians continued to be admired by healers down through the centuries. In fact, a turn-of-the century U.S. Government document, the Flexner Report, reinforced the value of treating illness vs. disease by implying that during the Civil War, patients would have had a better survival rate if they could have been treated by ancient Greek physicians instead of by trained American doctors.

As Christianity became more of a dominant force in Western medicine, the medical profession restricted its focus to physical disorders, influenced in part by the pervasive belief in mind-body dualism. The priest was entrusted with the care of the mind and soul, while the physician treated the material body. Thus arbitrary lines were drawn, the soul was split from the body, and this distinction became jealously guarded by both the priestly and medical professions. Crossing the mind/body barrier was severely punished. Spanish inquisitors, for example, took a dim view of medical autopsies. They considered such biological invasion as desecrating the temple of the soul and as a challenge to the Church's teachings explaining the nature and composition of man.

With the dawning of the seventeenth century came the development of science as we know it, a study of anatomy and physiology, and the precursor of nineteenth and twentieth Century biomedical reductionism. The modern biomedical model has evolved from such roots, a model which assumes disease to be fully explained by deviations from the norm of measurable biological/physical variables. This position embraces two principles:

1) **Reductionism,** which maintains that complex phenomena are ultimately derived from a single primary principle, i.e., physical.
2) **Mind/body dualism,** which distinguishes the mental/spiritual from the physical/material. Unfortunately, this philosophical position has caused medicine to stray from its holistic roots in its quest for scientific and technological advances in biology and to ignore the contributions of the behavioral and social sciences.

Much of early biomedicine, as a consequence, became preoccupied with disease at the expense of understanding and treating illness. Fortunately, twenty first century medicine is showing clear signs of appreciating that illness is more than a biological response. Illness is the patient's total response to disease, including the way sickness is perceived, labeled, experienced, expressed, and coped with by the patient and family. When the distinction between disease and illness is ignored or overlooked, a predictable confrontation occurs between patient and doctor. The doctor is primarily interested in the recognition and treatment of disease while the patient is concerned about illness problems, practical difficulties in living resulting from sickness, and their resolution. Tragically, with increasing technological sophistication, Western medicine, in its pursuit of the understanding and treatment of disease, has often lost the patient in the process.

Biopsychosocial Model

As an alternative to a strict biomedical model of health care, George Engel, a prominent 20th century physician, describes a biopsychosocial model. This model involves not only the examination of the relationship between biochemical processes and clinical data, but also focuses on a basic understanding of how patients communicate symptoms of disease within **psychological, social,** and **cultural** contexts. If Western medicine has a weakness, it might well be in the contradiction between the excellence of a physician's biomedical background and the constricted view of what it means to be ill. Some medical outcomes are inadequate not because appropriate technical interventions are lacking, but because the breadth of our conception of the patient may be too narrow.

So where is all this leading? When one fails to assess the patient's illness as well as disease, problems in health care delivery are predictable. The fix? Effective treatment can be facilitated by the doctor in **communicating within the patient's**

language and conceptual boundaries, understanding and respecting the patient's **explanatory model** (i.e., the patient's understanding of his illness), **negotiating** a mutually agreeable explanatory model and treatment plan, and **involving the patient** as an essential part of the treatment team.

Case Study in Biomedicine: Hap and Dr. Seitz

Early in my professional career, I had occasion to witness a tragic collision between disease and illness at the University of Colorado School of Medicine. It had been my privilege to work as a clinical psychology consultant to the organ transplant ward. While there, I had the opportunity to work with Colorado's first heart transplant, Hap, a former truck driver, proud father, devoted husband, and general character with a great sense of humor.

When I first met Hap, he was a strong-minded, independent, straight-talking fellow with a mind of his own and a determined sense of himself and the way he wanted to chart his life. He was Hap, take it or leave it. After several months in the hospital, however, his life became a different story. He was subjected to endless tests, blood drawings, injections, medications, observations, interviews, and what have you . . . all because he was Colorado's first heart transplant.

I last saw Hap at the University of Colorado's Grand Rounds, where I was involved in presenting part of his case to a packed audience of physicians, nurses, reporters, and the generally curious. Although Hap was there as a living tribute to the wonders of modern medicine, something seemed to be tragically missing. When Hap introduced himself to this crowd, I began to appreciate the difference between treating a person and a diseased biological part. The glaring difference between being a healer working with illness in contrast to a technician curing a disease became gut-wrenchingly clear . . . when this shadow of his former self said simply, "I am the heart." No more Hap. Just a body part.

SUMMARY AND KEY CONCEPTS

Your awareness of the differences between diagnosing and treating **disease** vs. **illness** helps patients like Hap heal. As you return to your reading of anatomy and physiology, consider a **biopsychosocial** perspective—a somewhat different vision that can compliment your study of medicine and your viable practice as a physician.

In reviewing this chapter, recall the significance of the following ideas:

1) Disease vs. illness
2) Mortality and behavior
3) The roots of the biomedical model: reductionism and dualism
4) Biomedicine and Hap: a case for the biopsychosocial approach

CHAPTER 3

LEARNING PRINCIPLES: THE "GUTS" OF BEHAVIORAL MEDICINE

Dorothy, an air traffic controller, appears in your office looking distraught and complaining of gastric pains.

"Doctor," she sighs, "my job is killing me. Last week the radar screen looked like an ant hill! Thank goodness no planes collided on my shift!"

She then changes the subject. "My stomach hurts but my family always seems to have had problems with their stomachs. Auntie Em continually complained about belly cramps and gas!"

Dorothy's look then becomes more somber. "My Dad would give anybody a pain in the gut. He is such a perfectionist! Nothing I do seems good enough for him! I'll never be worth much!"

"Doctor," she sighs again, "I think I might have made the mistake of the century in moving from Kansas to Seattle. I don't have any friends, my family seems thousands of miles away, and my dog Toto was stolen by a witch. When I'm not working, I just sit inside my trailer house in the rain . . . doing nothing."

Biopsychosocial Model

Let's consider a model, specifically a **biopsychosocial model,** that would take into account this patient's biology, her thoughts (cognitions), her behavior, her socio-cultural background and her environment—all interacting with each other! This model represents the complexity of factors and processes that influence patient as well as physician behavior, factors which **you need to be aware of** in order to make an accurate diagnosis and treatment plan for this patient's problems.

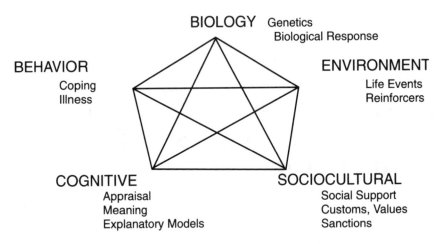

Figure 3-1:   A Biopsychosocial Model of Illness

Let's summarize Dorothy's situation. She is struggling with a very stressful job. She has a family history of excessive stomach acid release in response to stress (**biologically vulnerable**). Because of her past experience with a demanding, perfectionistic, critical father, she has excessively high personal standards and low self-esteem (**cognitively vulnerable**). To add to her problems, she is unmarried, has no family, has recently moved to a new city (**no social support**), and has no recreational pursuits (**no rewards or reinforcers**). The odds are very high that she will develop a gastrointestinal disorder in response to her stressful job situation. If you only prescribe Maalox, you've only done 20% of the treatment. Why?

Dorothy's clinical status might be likened to a computer. (It might also be likened to a character out of the *Wizard of Oz,* but that's another story.) Her **biology** provides the "hardware" underlying human behavior. Anatomy, physiology, genetics, and endocrine functions predetermine her biological vulnerability to certain disease or pathological processes. With this biological equipment, she interacts with the **environment** where she encounters potential stressors (e.g., life events such as job pressures, recently moving, dog theft etc. coupled with few rewards or recreational outlets combine to describe an environment for Dorothy that is decidedly "unfun"). Her **sociocultural** status isn't looking that promising either, with few family or friends to help buffer the wear and tear she is encountering.

The extent to which these events actually cause a stress response, however, is dependent not only upon the "hardware" (i.e., biology) but also on the "software" (i.e., **cognitive/perceptual** systems). How her potential stressors are processed through her **perceptual filter** determines how much wear and tear she will experience. Whether she perceives her "cup" as half full or half empty will have a decided impact on her stress response, including her body's response to such perceptions. That is, how she **appraises** her circumstances, what personal **meaning** these events have in her life, and how she interprets and **explains** them to herself will all have a significant bearing on how she **copes** with these stressors. The medical implications of such factors are of critical importance, as these responses to stressors can actually result in **illness.** It follows that treatment strategies, to be maximally effective, should focus upon all of these domains. The physician who focuses only upon the biologic, in effect, is ignoring 80% of his treatment possibilities.

Using this model to diagnose or analyze Dorothy's cognitive-perceptual-socio-cultural status (Wow! Look at us go crazy with hyphenated psychobabble!), as well as her physical pathology, you, as her doctor, can treat her by doing any or all of the following:

1) Reduce her **biological vulnerability** and her stress response through medication (e.g., antianxiety, hypertensive drugs, etc.).
2) Reduce or eliminate the appropriate **stressors** in her environment (e.g., changes in job situation, stress management exercises, physical exercise, etc.).
3) Reduce personal vulnerability and reduce stress by altering her **cognition** (i.e., modifying her maladaptive perceptions of the stressors and her own ability to cope with them).
4) Improve her **social support** (e.g., encourage the development of social, recreational and personal contacts).
5) Get her back to Kansas. (Just kidding!)

Your choices are, therefore, not restricted just to the use of drugs. But wait a minute. Why does Dorothy's stomach acid always get released by stress?—and how did she pick up all those beliefs about perfection and herself?—and how do all these things affect her behavior? Well, does the name "Pavlov" ring a bell? The answer is learning—all those connections in the diagram on page 12 are learned. To be more precise, they are conditioned, reinforced, and/or modeled, just to mention a few learning processes.

Take out your magic marker now, as we review some principles by which these learning processes take place. Most medical/behavioral problems that you will encounter in your practice will involve two types of learning: (1) classical (or respondent conditioning) and (2) operant conditioning.

Classical Conditioning

Classical conditioning refers to behavior that is elicited by a stimulus cue. For example, a physician (**conditioned stimulus**) who initially is not associated with any particular emotional reaction can become associated with an unpleasant procedure (**unconditioned stimulus**), which elicits pain (**unconditioned response**).

CS (physician) + **UCS** (unpleasant procedure) ⟶ **UCR** (Pain)

Figure 3-2: Classical Conditioning Process

After several exposures of the patient to these painful procedures, the physician alone soon elicits an unpleasant reaction (**conditioned response).**

CS (physician) $\longrightarrow$ **CR** (Unpleasant feeling)

Figure 3-3: Classically Conditioned Response

Recall the first couple of times you went to see the doctor and were given a shot. You didn't have to be a genius to come up with a thousand excuses to avoid walking through the good doctor's door a third time! Remember how you tried to put your feet into reverse when you caught the antiseptic smell of the waiting room! Cancer patients frequently exhibit conditioned nausea when they approach the hospital where they receive chemotherapy or radiation treatment. Can you explain why? Ivan Pavlov wrestled with these very issues when he conditioned his famous dogs to salivate in response to a bell. We humans do not seem to depart significantly from this animal paradigm, particularly in terms of learning emotionally driven responses.

Many emotional reactions, such as fear, are considered classically conditioned because they are elicited by antecedent stimulus cues. Effective behavioral techniques designed to reduce fears include systematic desensitization and its conceptual cousin, exposure therapy. We'll discuss these strategies later in our chapter, "Stress, Fear and Illness." But just to whet your appetite, **systematic desensitization** involves a three-step process:

1) Deep muscle relaxation
2) Construction of anxiety hierarchies (i.e., the patient identifying specific anxiety "triggers" or events which precipitate his fear)
3) Desensitization (i.e., pairing the anxiety-producing events with the patient's relaxation response)

Exposure therapy (which does not require relaxation training but does reduce anxiety by exposing the patient to the feared events) will be just the ticket to reduce some of Dorothy's woes, but you and she will have to wait a few pages longer, for, as Paul Harvey would say, "the rest of the story!" The clinical applications of classical conditioning can be helpful in anxiety reduction, but most health care problems lend themselves to modification through the second major type of learning, operant conditioning.

Operant Conditioning

We have seen that in classical conditioning, behavior is influenced by the stimuli that precede it, but in **operant conditioning,** behavior is influenced by what follows it (i.e., its consequences). This process was first discovered by Org, son of

Zog, who dropped a piece of prehistoric mastodon in his fire, fished it out of the flames in a medium-rare condition, ate it, and experienced a gustatory reward! Org, because of this positively reinforcing experience, continued to drop meat into the fire. The **consequences** of his meat dropping behavior, i.e., happy taste buds, reinforced his continuing to fling meat on the coals. The cave writings chronicle that not only did Org become the world's first prehistoric chef, but he also appears to have been the first Neanderthal behavioral scientist! Lest we stray too far from the point, however, the fundamental principle to be emphasized here is that **behavior is affected by its consequences**. Generally, it is the response to our behavior that determines whether or not we will continue that behavior. If the response is positive or rewarding, we say the behavior has been **reinforced** (strengthened, get it?) and will likely continue or increase.

The various types of reinforcers are outlined in the following figure:

	Behavior Increases	Behavior Decreases
Apply Stimulus	Positive Reinforcement (Reward)	Positive Punishment
Remove Stimulus	Negative Reinforcement	Negative Punishment 1. Extinction 2. Time Out 3. Response Cost (Fining)

Figure 3-4: Types of Reinforcement

Positive reinforcement refers simply to a reward (i.e., the presentation of a stimulus that increases the probability of the response it follows). **Negative reinforcement,** not to be confused with punishment, refers to the removal of an aversive stimulus which increases the probability of the response that preceded it In other words, stopping or avoiding something bad feels good (and increases the likelihood that the avoidance behavior will continue)! For example, an addict may inject himself with heroin not just because it feels good, but because the drug reduces or eliminates withdrawal symptoms such as stomach cramping, tremors, chills, etc. Therefore, the negative reinforcer, heroin, removes an aversive situation, stomach cramping, etc., and thereby increases the probability that heroin will be used again. There are basically two types of negative reinforcing behaviors: (1) **escape** from an unpleasant experience and (2) **avoidance** of an unpleasant experience.

Punishment, which involves the application of an aversive stimulus (e.g., a whack on the backside or a harsh word) to a behavior that one wants reduced or eliminated, usually results in a rapid reduction in that behavior. However, it carries with it some problematic side effects:

1) Punishment does not teach new behaviors, only the suppression of undesirable ones.

2) Such behavioral suppression caused by punishment is only temporary.
3) The punished typically avoid the punisher.
4) Behavioral rigidity results from punishment, producing a phenomenon called **learned helplessness.**
5) Negative emotional complications can occur in response to punishment, including aggression and disruptive emotional responses.
6) Punishment tends to reinforce the punisher, dissipating his anger and helping him feel like he is "getting even." Such personal gratification frequently blinds one to the impact that the punishment is having on the person being punished.

Punishment can be deceptive in its simplicity. It appears easy to use and is assumed to be obviously effective. Punishment is eagerly condoned by many subcultures as the "reinforcer of choice" because it's quick, decisive, and "feels good" to the dispensing agent. From a behavioral and learning perspective, however, there are reinforcement strategies that work much better than punishment and have fewer negative "side effects." More appropriate are three types of actions that decrease undesired behavior by removing the rewards for those behaviors:

1) **Extinction:** a process which removes a positive consequence for a specific activity. If a reward reinforces a behavior, then stopping the reward will likely stop the behavior. How long would you keep working if you stopped getting a paycheck? A behavior's resistance to extinction is a measure of its strength.

2) **Time out:** the elimination of all opportunities to earn reinforcement. You can become a legend in your own time by introducing time out concepts to young parents who are desperate in their attempts to effectively control temper tantrums in their children.

   Suggest to the "little nipper's" parents that they follow this procedure. First, "child proof" his room (i.e., remove breakable objects, etc.), put a lock on the door, and buy an egg timer. When he throws a tantrum, tell him he's going into "time out," and then gently, firmly, and silently (Don't argue with him!) take him to his room. Lock the door, set the timer for five minutes, and leave. When the bell rings after five minutes, open the door, and, if he has calmed down, let him out. If not, set the timer for five more minutes. When he is in time out, do **not** talk to him or provide him any attention . . . even if he offers to buy his parents a car, take them to Hawaii, totally reform his personality, or promises to behave. That can all happen after his five minutes are up. Create the mind-set in the parents that they should be prepared to repeat the five-minute drill for an hour. We've never had a child go beyond three five-minute segments at one time. Perhaps their child can set a record! More likely, however, temper tantrums will decrease, the parents will enjoy their child, and you will be a hero!

3) **Response Cost:** the forfeiture of rewards (i.e., fining or loss of privilege) when one misbehaves.

Response cost involves taking away rewards, **extinction** involves discontinuing reinforcers for a specific behavior, and **time out** refers to the temporary interruption of the availability of all reinforcement.

O.K. So you want to modify your own or someone else's behavior. Three basic steps are involved:

1) **Pinpoint:** Describe specifically, concretely and precisely the behavior to be modified (e.g., run 1 mile a day);
2) **Record:** Record the frequency or duration of the target behavior. This provides an accurate measure and a baseline to compare therapeutic change. (For example, you're starting at zero with your running program. No longer a slug!) A postscript: Self-monitoring of **un**wanted behavior can in and of itself reduce the frequency of such behavior.
3) **Reinforce:** Identify reinforcers and determine what particular reinforcers are manageable, controllable and powerful. Then define a reinforcement schedule and record the results. (e.g., Running a mile to the nearest convenience store for a beer was a clever twist. You're getting the idea!)

Now that you are familiar with the types of reinforcement, a word needs to be said about the conditions under which learning takes place. Certain conditions or "schedules" of reinforcement influence how quickly a behavior is learned and how resistant it is to extinction. Thus the **schedules of reinforcement** need to be assessed if we are to know how much effort will be required to teach a new behavior or unlearn an undesirable habit. When and in what pattern reinforcement is presented determines the rate of the response or behavior:

1) **Continuous reinforcement** occurs after every response. For example, a worker is paid for each shirt sewn. Behavior is initially learned most quickly with continuous reinforcement, but it also stops most quickly when reinforcement is stopped (remember extinction?).
2) **Fixed reinforcement** occurs after a set number of responses. For example, in a **fixed ratio schedule,** a worker is paid for every tenth shirt sewn. In a **fixed interval schedule,** a worker is paid every Friday, no matter how many shirts are sewn.
3) **Variable reinforcement** occurs after a random and unpredictable number of responses. Using the sewing example, a **variable ratio schedule** would be illustrated by payment in no predictable pattern, but on the average of every second, fifth, or tenth shirt sewn. A **variable interval schedule** would be demonstrated by an unpredictable payment schedule—like whenever the supervisor can afford to pay, no matter how many shirts are sewn. A used car salesperson on commission is a second illustration of such a schedule. Variable reinforcement schedules are quite resistant to extinction. Can you explain why?

If your vision is beginning to blur and your attention wander, give yourself some positive reinforcement **NOW!** You've hung in there with this material so far, so treat yourself to a sandwich, a cup of coffee, a stretch, or a brief break. We have just a few concepts left and you will have finished this chapter!

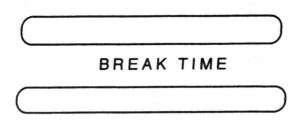

BREAK TIME

Welcome back! It wouldn't be medical school if you weren't asked to study a list or two! Behold some helpful behavioral medicine concepts.

Behavioral Principles

1) **Premack principle** (Grandma's Law): A high-frequency response (a behavior you enjoy) can be used as a reward or reinforcer for a low-frequency response (a behavior you don't enjoy). The principle is named for a psychologist (Premack), who learned it from his grandmother. As every Grandmother knows, "If you finish your homework or mow the lawn, you can watch television or go out and play."

2) **Token economy:** This technique is useful in teaching new behaviors in settings like mental hospitals, schools for the developmentally disabled, and, of course, employment in the free enterprise system. Desired behavior is rewarded with a token reinforcer that has acquired value (like the Yankee dollar). Tokens can then be exchanged for desired objects such as food, free time, Club Med, etc. Sounds a lot like our monetary system, wouldn't you say?

3) **Shaping:** Reinforcing graduated steps of successive approximations to the desired target behavior. For example, a young child learning to talk is rewarded for "Da," then "Dada," and finally "Daddy."

4) **Modeling:** What Cindy Crawford does for a living. Aha! Hope we didn't catch you napping! In the language of conditioning/learning, a desired behavior is modeled by a person of status—and that person's behavior is imitated and reinforced. Modeling is especially useful in teaching complex behaviors, like sports.

5) **Biofeedback:** An extension of operant conditioning in the electronic age. It is based on the premise that information is reinforcing. Through receiving electronic information (e.g., tone or visual display) about their body's functioning (e.g., muscle tension, perspiration, skin temperature, electroencephalogram readings, etc.), patients learn to recognize stress and ex-

ercise control over their physiologic reactions. Biofeedback involves three fundamental principles of learning/conditioning:

    a) The physiological parameter (e.g., muscle tension) must be **measurable.**
    b) The patient must receive **continuous information** about the physiological parameter.
    c) Mastery requires repetition or **practice.**

6) **Cognitive-behavioral therapy:** All of these principles are incorporated in a short-term method of psychotherapy that deals specifically with various forms of depression and anxiety. In addition to maladaptive behaviors, a patient's distorted, negative ways of thinking are challenged, reorganized, and replaced with more accurate and positive thoughts and beliefs.

7) **Bored-out-of-your-mind-from-reading-lists-omania:** A fortunately reversible psychological condition precipitated by studying too long. Take another break, relax, and spend some time with people who love you. If it worked for Dorothy, it can work for you. (She's back on the job directing air traffic, had her dog returned, and is working at a shelter for displaced scarecrows, tin persons, and lions!)

SUMMARY AND KEY CONCEPTS

Little did Dorothy know, as she entered your office, that she would be a walking/talking example of the biopsychosocial model and learning principles. Her case study combined the following biopsychosocial elements (Check out the "star" again on page 12):

1) **biology:** genetics and biological responses
2) **environment:** life events and reinforcers
3) **sociocultural:** social support, customs, values and sanctions
4) **cognitive:** perception, appraisal, meaning, and explanatory models
5) **behavioral:** coping and illness

These components of Dorothy's case blend into an interactive paradigm that can knock your medical socks off! What a gal!

Not to be outdone, the descendants of Ivan Pavlov described **classical (respondent) conditioning** as one of the two main learning strategies which will characterize your patients. After you straighten out the differences between conditioned and unconditioned stimuli and responses, you'll be well on your way to understanding the principles of two behavioral intervention strategies:

1) **Systematic desensitization**
    a) Relaxation training
    b) Construction of anxiety hierarchies
    c) Desensitization pairings

2) **Exposure therapy** (To be discussed when we get to the stress and fear chapter.)

Think of Org, the nimble Neanderthal who first demonstrated that in **operant conditioning,** behavior is learned and maintained by its consequences. Recall the three basic steps:

1) Pinpointing
2) Recording
3) Reinforcing

Org's first conditioning experiences were primitive, but he ate well!

Now review the Reinforcement chart on page 15. It should take the mystery out of understanding the different **kinds of reinforcers:**

1) Reward or positive reinforcement
2) Negative reinforcement
3) Positive punishment
4) Negative punishment
   a) Extinction
   b) Time out
   c) Response cost.

Schedules of Reinforcement are always a hot item around exam time, so remember **fixed vs. variable** and **ratio vs. interval** and combine them to your heart's content. Confused? See page 17. Don't overlook such helpful learning concepts as:

1) Grandma's Law
2) Token economy
3) Shaping
4) Modeling
5) Biofeedback
6) "Other" (Doesn't that just drive you nuts! "Other" must be important because its always on the test!) Kidding again, but if your sense of humor is shot, go out and have a burger in memory of Org. If you've done your reading effectively, you should now be feeling the relaxing effects from the study break on page 18. If you ignored such wisdom, jump to the chapter on stress management. . . you need it!

CHAPTER 4

PSYCHODYNAMIC PSYCHOLOGY: BLACK BOXES AND BAND-AIDS

Throughout medical history, physicians have struggled to understand what makes their patients "tick." The behavioral approach (described in the last chapter), developed by B.F. Skinner and others, maintained that to understand and predict human behavior, one need only understand the **stimulus** and **response** characteristics of a person's behavior (Stimulus-Response Model). That is, behavior is influenced by stimulus conditions (antecedents), responses, and the effects of those responses (consequences). Little attention was paid to the mechanisms (e.g., neuro-endocrine) that linked stimulus to response. These aspects of the patient remained a "black box." One did not need to study what was in the "black box" between the stimulus and response, i.e., the "personality."

The behavioral position stood in dramatic contrast to the psychodynamic model of the nineteenth and early twentieth century, developed primarily by Sigmund Freud, the father of Psychoanalysis. To Freud, by training a neurologist, what occurred in the "black box" was all important. Human behavior was only the tip of the intrapsychic iceberg, the main mass of which lay deep within the person's unconscious. For Freud, physicians needed to look beyond observably obvious behavior into the personal or symbolic meaning of behavior. The intrapsychic world did not play by logical rules. In the "black box" of our inner selves

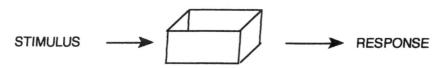

STIMULUS   →   RESPONSE

Figure 4-1: Stimulus-Response Model and the "Black Box"

raw emotion held sway, only obliquely governed by syllogistic reasoning, mores, sanctions and reality.

Psychoanalytic Intrapsychic Topography

Freud's landscape of the mind's "black box" has three levels:

1) **Unconscious:** A vast repository of repressed thoughts and feelings driven by primary process thinking. This type of thinking does not follow logical steps, has little contact with reality, and does not bend to the dictates of cause and effect. The unconscious is fueled by the energy of primitive drives, including the hunger for pleasure and wish fulfillment.
2) **Preconscious:** This level contains memories that are readily recalled. The type of thinking at this level is logical and reality-based.
3) **Conscious:** This part of the psyche does make direct connection with the external environment around us but does not have direct contact with the unconscious.

Consider an illustration. As you read these words, your awareness of your reading is an example of a conscious act. Reflecting on what you had for breakfast today is a preconscious function. You were not aware of today's breakfast until I called your attention to it, and then the details were available to your awareness. Ready for a challenge? Reflect on the last time you had sensual thoughts about your parent of the opposite sex. Bizarre? You don't remember having such thoughts? Freud would maintain that we all have had such thoughts—for men, the **Oedipus Conflict** and for women, the **Electra Complex**—both central concepts in the development of relations with the opposite sex and sometimes the basis for the development of neuroses. The reason you don't recall such feelings, Freud would argue, is because such feelings are unconscious and therefore not available to your awareness through ordinary means. In classical Psychoanalysis, however, through the use of free association and dream interpretation, the analyst may assist the patient in uncovering unconscious conflicts through well-timed interpretations. Now back to Freud's description of the psyche.

Intrapsychic Structures of Psychoanalysis

Within this psychological topography, Freud postulated a three-part functional theory of the mind:

1) **Id:** The "Tasmanian devil" of our psyche, the "seething cauldron of psychic impulses," including sexual/pleasure-seeking and aggressive drives, which know no logical control. The id runs *via* primary process thinking, acts in concert with the pleasure principle, and is not directly influenced by exter-

nal reality. Like the Tasmanian devil, the uncontrolled id sweeps through the universe, attempting to devour all in its path, often not discriminating between eating a bunny rabbit or a boulder . . . its all the same to the id.

2) **Ego:** Saving us from certain id-driven destruction is the ego, Freud's psychic function which controls our drives by adapting to the demands of reality. The ego is our reality tester.

3) **Superego:** Assisting the ego in controlling the id, this function of the mind consists of two parts:

   a) **Ego ideal:** The expectations, values and ideals for which we strive.

   b) **Conscience:** The "angel" in our psyche who provides us the moral and legal guidelines within which we act socially responsibly.

Note that the superego represents the influences of family, society and culture.

Defense Mechanisms

Within this complex interplay of competing forces and needs, the human psyche has its work cut out for it. The ego develops techniques, some unconscious, to resolve, modify or ignore conflicts. These techniques are designed to decrease anxiety and maintain a person's sense of safety, balance and self-esteem. Such strategies, termed **ego defense mechanisms,** include the following:

Denial: Parts of reality are refused recognition in favor of one's own fantasies.

Displacement: A person redirects an emotion from its original object to a more comfortable substitute.

Identification: Characteristics of another are taken on as one's own.

Intellectualization: A person rationalizes, shifting from a focus on inner conflicts to abstract ideas.

Projection: A person's own unacceptable feelings are disowned and attributed to another.

Reaction Formation: Repressed motives are translated into their opposites.

Regression: A person partially returns to an earlier stage of development in which life is more "user friendly" and one's coping mechanisms prove more effective.

Repression: Unacceptable impulses or experiences are unconsciously excluded from awareness.

Sublimation: Unacceptable feelings are converted or redirected to more socially sanctioned outlets.

Suppression: Unpleasant thoughts, feeling, or experiences are consciously pushed from awareness, i.e., "I'm putting this out of my mind."

Undoing: One attempts to negate or annul some unacceptable thought or action.

Case Study in Ego Defense Mechanisms

How about a flesh-and blood case that exemplifies and hopefully clarifies some of these concepts?

Ben Bandaid, superstar in his undergraduate years at Smalltown College, finally arrived at the University of WHAMO School of Medicine for his first year of med school.

As he walked to his first day of class, Ben muttered to himself, "Life is going to be a total piece of cake in this place!" **[Denial]**

Tension began to creep into his body as he tried not to think about all the work he was about to take on. **[Suppression]** He was beginning to feel terrified.

He passed a fellow medical student, noting to himself, "She really looks scared stiff!" **[Projection]**

Ben failed to acknowledge his own hands trembling and his stomach churning, experiences possibly precipitated by having been traumatized in the second grade by getting his first and only "B." This memory, however, had long been tucked away in the inner recesses of his unconscious. **[Repression]**

He crossed the crowded campus to the Registrar's Office, where an unpleasant lady with blue hair told him that his registration packet had been lost and there was no record of any Ben Bandaid ever having been accepted to medical school. He was furious, but looked at the woman and reminded himself that she was simply doing her job. **[Intellectualization]** He smiled at her, thanked her for her efforts, and reached out warmly to shake her hand. **[Reaction Formation]** Betty Bluehair stared at Ben coldly, rejected his hand, and curtly hissed at him to get out of the long line so that she could help others.

As he started to leave the office, he accidentally bumped the next student in line. Ben said nothing but glanced at this student thinking, "You clumsy son-of-a-bitch!" **[Displacement]**

Catching himself overreacting to this nudge, he patted the bumped student on the shoulder, saying, "Sorry, guy! Didn't mean to hit you." **[Undoing]**

Ben was so wired from his Registrar's Office debacle that he thought he could fly on his own power. His anger bubbled on the edge of control as he sputtered to himself and took a detour to the gym. He dressed in his running clothes and tried to break the four-minute mile with all of his pent up frustration and energy. **[Sublimation]**

As he raced around the indoor track, he thought about his physician father whom Ben dearly admired and loved. "Dad said that there would be days like this, but he made it. Guess I can too!" **[Identification]**

After such psychoanalytic aerobics, is there any doubt that Ben is on his way to a successful medical career?! His Dad (and Sigmund Freud) would be proud!

SUMMARY AND KEY POINTS

Within the tri-level realm of the psyche (**conscious, preconscious** and **unconscious**), Freud postulated three functions: **id, ego** and **superego,** the last having two components, ego ideal and conscience. Note how these functions interact. The ego develops strategies or defense mechanisms to help the psyche defend against anxiety/fear. Soon-to-be Dr. Ben Bandaid illustrated 11 of these mechanisms. If the formal definitions of these mechanisms are still confusing to you, revisit Ben's story. And for your memory's consideration, here's an alphabetical listing of the **defense mechanisms:**

Denial
Displacement
Identification
Intellectualization
Projection
Reaction Formation
Regression
Repression
Sublimation
Suppression
Undoing

Need some memory hooks? Start free associating to this list. See what you can come up with. And as they say in the Analytic biz, "Sweet dreams"!

CHAPTER 5

DOCTOR-PATIENT COMMUNICATION: HEALING WORDS

The pained and embarrassed expression of the post-mammectomy patient still haunts us, as she haltingly asks the surgeon about the scars from her incisions, which were held together by a row of surgical-steel staples.

"Tell your husband," smirks the surgeon, "that you'll look just like a Playboy centerfold, and you'll have the staple-marks to prove it!"

Perhaps the surgeon was trying to be funny to lighten the tension in the examining room. Maybe he was too exhausted to be sensitive to his anxious patient and her concerns. Whatever the reason, his attempt at humor ladened with sarcasm created a psychological chasm between doctor and patient that might never be bridged. What remained was a collapsed communication and fractured relationship between them.

Upon viewing this vignette in the film, *The Doctors*, our first year medical school class couldn't believe that this was anything other than a caricature, an example of a "bad doctor" which none of them would ever become. Yet one of the students noted, "Even after just three months of medical school, we are already being set apart from other people. We are learning a specialized vocabulary, fancy Greek words that describe our anatomy, and when we use them, only our 'in group' understands." And this sense of professional "difference" continues to evolve through one's medical and professional education. The potential barriers it can create in your communication with patients is what this chapter is all about.

A little-known, gray-haired doctor was once quoted as saying, "The most valuable tool that I have as a healer is the relationship between me and my patient." Such a statement seems a bit difficult to swallow in this age of CAT scans and high-tech medicine. Surely something as mundane as a relationship (and something as simple as communication) can hardly compete with the healing arsenal of Western medicine. Well, we'll see. In fact, research demonstrates repeatedly the critical role effective communication and the doctor-patient relationship play in clinical practice. In a word, no communication and no relationship, no healing. An overstatement? Think about it! The surgery was a success, but the patient died. In our chapter on biopsychosocial medicine we talked about transplanting "the heart" but losing "Hap," the person. We cured the disease but ignored the illness. A breast can be stapled together after cancer surgery, but fractured and insensitive physician communication does not heal the patient! Off the soapbox for a bit. Story time.

Non-adherence and Treatment Failure

Dr. Stewart is furious. Clem, his middle-aged liver problem, is ignoring his directive to stop drinking.

"Damn it, Clem! You're not paying any attention to what I'm trying to tell you! Listen to me. Either you stop drinking **now,**" the doctor emphasizes with his fist banging down on his desk, "or you're a dead man! This booze is killing you!"

Clem slowly rises from his chair as he gets to his feet, puts on his soiled cowboy hat, and looks squarely at the physician.

"Well, Doc," he says in his Montana drawl, "I know a hell of a lot more old drunks than old doctors!"

Non-adherence to medical treatment is a major cause of treatment failure. It also is one of the largest and heaviest crosses to bear for the practicing physician. A host of excuses precipitates non-adherence:

1) Medical advice may not be compatible with patients' other social roles or expectations:
   "Doc, I haven't got time for this therapy. I have a business to run."
2) The physician's advice may be inconsistent with the advice of patients' friends and family:
   "Marge said at our bridge club that Prozac causes cancer and stu . . . stu . . . stuttering!"
3) Patients and/or their families may not like the physician, the bill, the bedside manner, or some other aspect of their medical care:
   "My doctor's heart is as cold as his instruments and his wallet."

Misperceptions, along with amazing irrational fantasies, can blossom on the part of the physician as well as the patient. These misperceptions and fantasies contribute to difficult and strained doctor-patient relationships. What to do? The primary solution to non-adherence is effective and accurate communication. Examine what's going on with your communication!

Therapeutic Relationships

Where to start? How about at the foundation of all solid relationships—**friendship.** We could wax eloquently about the components of effective relationships, but by now you have developed a sophisticated sense, at least intuitively, about what stable friendships, be they personal or professional, are all about. You know what it takes to be a friend. An obvious point, but regularly overlooked.

Supporting some of your intuitive ideas of what an effective relationship is all about, Dr. Carl Rogers, founder of Client-Centered Therapy and a pioneer researcher in psychotherapy, discussed the importance of several factors in a truly **therapeutic relationship:**

1) **Be genuine,** i.e., personable, friendly, and "real."
2) Extend yourself through **empathic understanding,** getting a feel for what it's like to walk in the other's footsteps. Empathy involves hearing and understanding the patient in the patient's own terms, communicating that understanding to the patient, and the patient accurately receiving your communication.
3) **Accept** (which does not necessarily mean agree with) patients' points of view, acknowledging in a caring and respectful manner their personal dignity, even though we may disagree with their opinions and behavior.

In examining the doctor-patient relationship, consider the **channels of communication** which are used to make psychological contact with one another: (1) *Facial expressions;* (2) *Body language;* and (3) *Speech.* Its helpful to focus on not only your words, but how you say them (your tone, intensity, and volume etc.).

Levels of Communication

Interpersonal communication occurs on a continuum. All communication might be viewed as occurring on three levels: (1) cognitive; (2) emotional; and (3) transactional.

1) **Cognitive level:** Cognitive communication is characterized as logical, intellectual thinking with the focus on content. You as a physician have access to this level by simply listening to the words the patient is speaking. Cognitive/intellectual communication strategies include the following:
   a) **Silence:** This is indeed a communication technique, although communication is being conducted primarily through nonverbal channels. The critical question with regard to silence is, "What does it mean?" The reasons for silence must be inferred. Through her silence, your patient might be indicating some self-examination, seeking new insights,

considering new directions to take the conversation, or perhaps wishing to avoid a topic. When silence is used by the physician, the effect is twofold: (1) it slows down the pace of an interview; and (2) if you are attentive, communicates your undivided interest in what the patient is trying to say.

b) **Phrases:** Using several word comments such as "uh huh," or "I see" will help reinforce or encourage the patient to continue her discussion.

c) **Restatement:** Paraphrasing what has already been said using similar words signals your understanding and encourages the patient to explain further.

d) **Questions:** Inquiries designed to determine **what, where, when, why** and **how** can be used to further explore the patient's problems so as to arrive at some possible solutions. In most clinical settings, questions are overused, but they can prove to be very powerful tools in understanding the patient's clinical circumstances. Questions can generate anxiety for your patient. However, if used correctly, open-ended questions, sensitively and tactfully put, can be used to establish rapport and construct an emotional bridge between doctor and patient.

Indeed, there is a real art in asking effective questions. For example, if you are attempting to determine how successful a particular set of treatment instructions has been, you might ask, "Do you understand?" Of course, the obvious answer will generally be "Yes", whether the patient understands or not. However, if you were to ask your patient to tell you, in her own words, what she is expected to do, you might find such a question provides more accurate and helpful information about her understanding of your treatment instructions.

2) **Emotional level:** As you are aware from your own experience, a person's emotional responses intend to enrich the message as well as modify it. Emotions provide you access not only to the events of a patient's world, but also to his reactions to these events. When you want to enter a patient's emotional country, the initial focus of your journey should be to reflect your patient's feelings, mirroring them in a way that not only captures the content, but also the intensity of the communication.

"Wait a minute," you say, "feelings tend to be messy at times and can slow down my busy appointment schedule." However, when you adequately capture the emotional expression of your patient, this will substantially reduce his level of stress. Reflecting feelings tends to diminish the intensity of such feelings. Further, reflecting feeling tends to communicate, on your part, warmth, compassion and understanding. When you have accurately reflected your patient's feeling state, notice how his tension and apprehension dissipate. He begins to accept his own experiences, thereby reducing internally perceived stress-producing conflicts. In the end, you have moved more quickly to the treatment goal and actually saved time.

How is reflection of feeling accomplished?

a) **Listen.** Consider the example of a woman who has been told that she probably will need surgery. As she begins to cry, you have several options. You can tell her crying won't help. Or ask her why she is crying. Perhaps the most emotionally effective approach, however, would be for you to simply allow her to cry without interruption and then acknowledge her distress. This more personal response will also create a positive climate for you to ask more clinical questions. Note, too, that once an accepting emotional/personal climate has been established, a patient tends to give more accurate and in-depth responses to clinical questions.

b) **Reflection of feeling** or "emotional paraphrasing." On a cognitive level, paraphrasing is restatement. In a restatement, one uses different words to mirror the content of the communication. When communication is on an emotional level, however, emotional paraphrasing involves more "gut-level" talk, mirroring more emotion than word content. For example, if a patient were to say, "Boy, am I anxious!" you might comment, "You sound *really* uptight!" When such a statement is adequately punctuated by voice tone, pitch, volume, and tension, the emotional nuances of your paraphrasing are brought to the forefront. The intent, therefore, in reflection of feeling is to mirror what the patient is saying on an emotional level.

c) **Colorful speech and analogies,** if consistent with the patient's culture and vocabulary, can serve you well as a powerful technique. Using the preceding example of the anxious patient, you might say, "You sound like you are wound up like an eight-day alarm clock" or, "You seem to feel under so much pressure that you could almost circle this room and bounce off the walls!" These somewhat colorful analogies might well capture the emotional tone of what this patient is trying to convey. Her affirmative response will let you know that you have captured the depth of her feeling. When her eyes begin to moisten and she looks gratefully at you because of your understanding, you have connected squarely with her psyche!

3) **Transactional level:** This level of communication requires a brief explanation of Transactional Analysis' view of our personality. Not unlike Freud's id, ego, and superego, the TA model postulates the "child," "adult" and "parent" as principal players in Everyman's psyche. Schematically, the TA model looks like three circles stacked on each other:

O [Parent]
O [Adult]
O [Child]

Figure 5-1: TA Model of Personality

When two people, such as a doctor and patient, engage in communication, a number of transactions are possible:

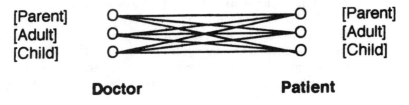

Figure 5-2:   Possible Transactions in TA Model

When both doctor and patient are communicating on the same level, generally there are few problems. When cross transactions occur, however, duck! That is, when the doctor's Parent is hooking the patient's Child (e.g., lecturing the "naughty boy" for not taking his blood pressure pills), communication gets plugged. Or when the patient's Child is throwing a tantrum at the doctor's Parent (e.g., "I hate these damn pills and you can't make me take them! So there!"), we have some major communication problems. The therapeutic strategy in such situations is to rebalance the communication so that eventually both parties are on the same wavelength, talking on an Adult-to-Adult level.

With this brief peek into the complex world of doctor-patient communications, each level of interaction seems to have its pro's and con's. If you choose to respond on a **cognitive level,** several results appear likely:

1)   Patient problem solving and decision making can be enhanced;
2)   The patient may find it easier to make plans; and
3)   The patient who is easily threatened by feelings may feel less anxious and more relieved.

When you choose to respond on an **emotional level,** one might expect several possibilities, including:

1)   The intensity of the patient's feelings may diminish;
2)   The patient is helped in incorporating experiences into her self concept; and
3)   You are likely to be perceived by the patient as communicating warmth, caring and concern about her well being.

From a **transactional level,** when you choose to communicate from a Parent position, you have a good chance of being perceived as a person in authority who is competent and should be listened to. But like a father or teacher, a Parent role has its down side, as any teenager will tell you (with much glee)! If you communicate from your inner Child, the good news is that such a transaction can be filled with humor, joy, and just plain fun. The bad news is that our Child can also exaggerate, can be wanting on the follow-through, and can be unpredictable in his immaturity. The Adult position isn't perfect either, but at least doctor and patient are on an emotionally level playing field in a game that is governed by the rules of logic—a good place to begin a healthy communication pattern! Effective adult communication surely beats having a relationship ripped open by misunderstanding and hurt feelings, and then trying to staple its fractured parts back together again.

SUMMARY AND KEY CONCEPTS

We have explored in this chapter the ravages of insensitive communication and non-adherence as well as some components of effective communication:
Ingredients for an effective **therapeutic relationship** or friendship include:

1) Genuineness
2) Empathic understanding
3) Acceptance

In sending messages to our patients, we use **channels of communication** which involve:

1) Facial expression
2) Body language
3) Speech

Doctor-patient interaction occurs on a continuum, a continuum which taps several **levels of communication** and their respective **strategies:**

1) Cognitive
   a) Silence
   b) Phrases
   c) Restatement
   d) Questions
2) Emotional
   a) Listen
   b) Reflection of feeling
   c) Colorful speech and analogies
3) Transactional
   a) Identification of transaction level for both doctor and patient.
   b) Move toward the same level of transaction, preferably the Adult-Adult level.

And a final thought: Communication is an essential tool for the healer. Don't leave home without it!

CHAPTER 6

MEDICAL CARE AND THE FAMILY: THE MYTH OF THE MARLBORO MAN

Return once again to Neolithic times. Org has just completed his meal of semi-cooked mastodon steak. Having reduced his basic drives for food and drink, he begins ascending his hierarchy of needs, arriving at "preservation of the species." That very evening, Org and his mate Orga start the steps necessary toward beginning a family, not having a clue as to what ramifications this venture will have on generations to follow. Nine months later, this couple beholds Orgette, their first daughter, who catapults them from couplehood into "the family way!" Not long afterward they postulate the **Neolithic First Law of Human Behavior:**

"Insanity is inherited. You get it from your kids."

They further discover that nothing is more complex and challenging than intimate family relationships . . . nothing! That includes astrophysics and discovering fire.

Eons later, the imminent American family therapist Virginia Satir illustrates the complex interactions among family members by a simple exercise: She asks family members to fasten themselves together with a rope and then be aware of how each person's movement affects everyone else. It's virtually impossible to make any movement that does not impact the others. **The point:** As family we are all connected, like it or not.

Behavior does not occur in a vacuum, and neither does illness. A patient is not an island unto himself. In spite of the attention given to the Marlboro Man, who projects the image of a rugged individualist who doesn't need anybody but his horse and a cigarette, people need people. Psychologist George Mead, an early 20th century personality theorist, maintains that our personal identity is equal to the sum total of our interpersonal relationships. No relationships, no identity. Although such a position may be an overstatement, it nonetheless emphasizes the role other people play in our lives, including our illnesses. If people in general are considered important to our sense of self, our families play an even more central role in the architecture of our lives, including how we perceive and cope with illness.

We learn about illness and health from our families. Orgette will learn from her Dad that the swamp spirit produces vapors that bring sickness. She will also learn that tossing her first bite of mastodon meat into the swamp to please this spirit may keep sickness away or at bay. If you, as a prehistoric shaman, were to treat Orgette for pneumonia, it might serve you well to respect the Org family lore surrounding illness before you give her a shot of antibiotic. Superstition can be stronger than science. Orgette's **family can be a valuable resource and source of support** in your treatment, or a powerful force undercutting your efforts.

To the present day, the role of family continues to loom powerfully in the perception and treatment of illness. Research consistently validates the healing effects of **family support** during illness. Involving the family in the care and treatment of one of it's members dramatically increases your ability to manage your patient's illness effectively. Understanding the **role and function** within the family that a member's illness serves can also be important, because sometimes physical symptoms can actually be adaptive in helping the family system operate! In certain families, parental conflicts are shunted through an ill child, resulting in less stress for the parents (the adaptive part of this strategy) but more stress and illness for the child (the pathological component of this strategy). Family therapy has proven helpful in resolving such family patterns. For example, in the preceding case therapy may focus on reducing parental conflicts without having to stress the child.

Within our families we learn how to survive emotionally and prosper beyond illness and health. We learn how to nurture and love. But it's virtually impossible to love when we are in pain. Adolescent Orgette, having developed a drinking problem, may smash up against parental authority and make life hell for her family. In such a pickle, however, she may be like a girl with a whopping toothache—she can think of only two things: her pain and seeking pain-relief. In pain, she can't love anyone, including herself. Many times symptoms presented within a family are simply failing coping strategies originally designed to keep members from hurting more.

The family, as the preceding examples imply, is a **system.** It is a system made up of subgroups who create boundaries that define "who does what to whom." As one tries to keep balanced in the "family mobile," one can become overinvolved in relationships or become detached and distant. Either extreme weighs down one part and throws the whole mobile out of equilibrium. It's important to understand that the **intent** of such patterns is to **improve** one's predicament. That may be the result **in the short haul,** but, unfortunately, such actions have negative effects over time. The short-term "remedies" may be borrowed from our familial past, representing solutions that once worked but may now be out of date and ineffective.

The story is told of a daughter who was preparing a ham for Thanksgiving dinner. Before the daughter put it into the roasting pan, her mother told her to cut three inches off the end. When the daughter asked why, her mother told her to ask her grandmother. Granny was consulted and referred them to her mother, the ancient and wise great-grandmother, who was resting in the living room.

"Great granny," the daughter asked, "why do you cut three inches off the Thanksgiving ham?"

"Because when I was cooking hams," the elderly lady replied, "My roasting pan was three inches too short!"

Like trimming the ham, illness symptoms, pathological from today's perspective, may have been functional and adaptive in earlier generations. Such behaviors include not only physical symptoms, but emotional and interpersonal responses as well (e.g., communication patterns, arguing styles, ways of showing intimacy, etc.). Diagnosing what factors maintain these symptoms is central to effective intervention. Important diagnostic questions include:

1) What interactions are occurring in the family which reinforce these behaviors?
2) Who communicates to whom, when, about what, in what circumstances, and for what purposes?
3) What **stresses** are bearing down on the family?
                finances
                work
                relationship problems
                empty nest divorce
                separation
                death
                child custody and visitation
                single-parenting
                blended families
4) What family resources can be used to transform problems into solutions?

Family communication patterns can become more muddled under stress. Within a relationship, each person may think the other seems to speak a foreign language: "I talk in practical German and she babbles in emotional French!" A popular book describing the differing patterns of communication between sexes speaks of men being from Mars and women from Venus. Stir these sexual communication differences into a melting pot of "in-laws vs. the outlaws" (i.e., his side vs. her side of the family), and the outcome is a Tower of Babel that would challenge the United Nations' ability to interpret what each person in the relationship is communicating to the other!

Perhaps the most challenging part of family communication involves the emotional undertones spoken "between the lines." A subtle look, a raised eyebrow, a phrase slightly twisting an emotional knife blade, a tone of voice slipping by logical defenses—such are the "vibes" that try one's soul as we try to communicate with each other. For example, trying to "make logical and reasonable" the emotional agenda that flies around during holiday times can be like trying to hit a home run in the World Series when all you have played is sandlot baseball. You are psychologically batting against world-class pitching with some of the relatives, and try as you will, the score probably will always be 9 to 3. Guess who is on the short end of the score . . . and will continue to be. Solution: Enjoy scoring three, respect the person who has scored nine, and consider negotiating a shift to a different sport or playing field!

As family dynamics impacting health problems become more complex, consider "calling in the cavalry" by referring to professionals familiar with dysfunctional family patterns. When family-embedded illness behaviors do not respond to primary health care, discretion can become the better part of valor. Red flags indicating referral include:

> Chronic depression or anxiety
> Significant suicidal risk
> Alcohol or drug dependence
> Long term family problems
> Spouse and child abuse
> Long term personality disorders

There is no shame in referring challenging family problems, particularly when the dynamics are interfering with proper medical care. If the Marlboro Man stumbles in his attempt to survive alone, maybe there's a moral: Medicine need not be a lonely business. We need to consult with colleagues, especially concerning dysfunctional families.

SUMMARY AND KEY CONCEPTS

From Neolithic times to the present day practice of medicine, certain facts about families appear in evidence:

1) Within our families, we are all **connected.** No one is an island.
2) We learn sick and well behaviors from our families. Illness typically serves a **role** and **function** within the family system.
3) A patient's family can be a **source of support and healing,** or a divisive force undercutting treatment.
4) The family is a **system** which is highly resistant to change. It may have outdated and counterproductive "survival styles". Like preparing the Thanksgiving ham, family ways of nurturing its members may need revision in terms of:
   a) Communication patterns
   b) Arguing styles
   c) Sharing affection and intimacy
5) Assessing family **stress** and its impact on members can provide the opening for transforming problems into solutions.

To summarize our point about the importance of seeking **consultation** when dealing with a challenging family, permit us to wax poetically:

> In complex family conflicts
> When the score is 9 to 3
> It's not poor form to wring your hands.
> Call in the cavalry!

SECTION II

CLINICAL PROBLEMS

CHAPTER 7

STRESS, FEAR AND ILLNESS: TIGERS, CAVES, AND COPING

Around two million years ago, Org (remember him?) was returning home to his cave when he was confronted by a saber-toothed tiger. "F-f-f-f-f-f!" Org stuttered. Fortunately his arms and legs required no translation, as he quickly **fled** the scene. Not to be outdone, however, the tiger raced after Org, backing him into a corner. Org drew his club, **fought** the tiger, and saved the day and himself. Later that afternoon, Org recorded these events on his cave wall, producing the first known documentation for man's **fight or flight (F-f) response** in the face of stress.

Even in our own century, the symbolic "saber-toothed tiger" lives, at least in spirit, as he prowls our streets and psyches in the form of various threats and challenges—final exams, unpaid bills, sulking boyfriends, and bad hair days! And this seemingly immortal tiger still creates "stress," the buzzword of the nineties, among the masses. Elixirs for stress are touted from the *Reader's Digest* to the *New England Journal of Medicine*. Muscled TV personalities hype exercise machines, diets, health foods, and other products to help us win the battle with stress. But what is stress? What does it do to us? What can we do about it?

Stress and the General Adaptation Syndrome

Hans Selye, a Canadian pioneer in research physiology, first talked about stress as a nonspecific or general response of our body to demands made on it. More simply, he described stress as wear and tear. Selye suggested that our body's nonspecific attempt to defend itself against threat occurs in three stages of the **General Adaptation Syndrome** (G.A.S.): (1) alarm, (2) resistance, and (3) exhaustion.

1) **Alarm stage:** When the stressor is first encountered, the sympathetic portion of our autonomic nervous system goes bananas, releasing epinephrine and a lot of other things. Sugars and fats pour into the bloodstream to provide fuel for quick energy. We breathe more rapidly, with red blood cells flooding our circulatory system, moving oxygen quickly to our muscles, arms and legs, and brain. Our heart rate quickens, our blood pressure surges, and our general body systems mobilize for one heck of a fight or one amazing flight! Digestion stops, sweat and salivation increase, our endocrine system accelerates hormonal production as adrenalin pours into our system. Don't be surprised if your eyes bug out, your pupils dilate, and the ol' stomach, bowel and bladder muscles give you fits. Many an alarm reaction has been punctuated with pains in the gut and soiled jeans! Flight or Fight responses can be hard on the body!

   For Org, it only took two or three encounters with the saber-toothed tiger before the very word "tiger" (translated from Neanderthal) or even a low growl would set off all those autonomic responses inside him. This conditioned autonomic fear response had survival value, but it soon was set off any time Org found himself in a challenging situation.

2) **Resistance:** The organ adjustments designed to cope immediately with the stressor begin to tire over time. Org's organ systems start to poop out!

3) **Exhaustion:** The collapse of resistance, an organismic breakdown, generally in response to prolonged stress, resulting in increasing wear and tear on the body (e.g., ulcers, hypertension, headaches, etc.) and even death. In summarizing the above process, Org might well have said, "When life is a G.A.S. (General Adaptation Syndrome) you A.R.E. (alarmed, resist, and exhausted)!"

Stress and Illness

Now the bad news. When life is a G.A.S., and your resistance and adaptation falter, illness can result. The research is clear in establishing a connection between stress and illness, although the relationship is not linear or absolute (i.e., Not everyone who experiences stress develops an illness, nor will leading a low stress life always guarantee good health). However, stress is a major player in the development of peptic ulcer disease, hypertension, some forms of cancer, immune system disorders and psychiatric illness.

The role of stress has been especially emphasized in coronary artery disease. Friedman and Rosenman first noted the relationship between heart attacks and certain personality factors which they described in 1959 as the Type A Behavior Pattern: Sense of time urgency, impatience, competitiveness, and hostility. Thank goodness none of these characteristics lurk around medical school!

Holmes and Rahe, in their classic studies at the University of Washington, established direct relationships between the **number and the degree** of life changes and the **risk and magnitude** of illness. In their research they quantified life events, assigning different weights to those events which they described as **life change units** or LCU's. At the top of the list was death of a spouse, assigned a value of 100. They gave such life events as marital separation a value of 65, marital reconciliation a value of 45, and vacation a value of 13. Even Christmas received a value of 12. Many of the activities that we cherish and truly enjoy nevertheless generate a good deal of wear and tear. Stress, therefore, can be **both** positive and negative.

Holmes and Rahe concluded that:

1) Life events which require changes in lifestyle are associated with the onset of illness.
2) Life change is a necessary but not sufficient cause of disease.
3) A direct correlation exists between the magnitude of life change and the likelihood of illness. (Patients with LCU's exceeding 300 may have an 80% chance of suffering from minor illness.)
4) Life change magnitude correlates directly both with the **risk** and the **severity** of illness.

Mediators of the Stress Response

For Org, and for you, two important factors influence your response to these life changes: your **perceptions** (or the meaning you assign to the stressor) and your **social support:**

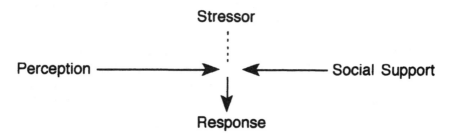

Figure 7-1:   Factors Influencing Stress Response

Each of us looks at reality through our own individualized "perceptual filter." We are "programmed" by our experiences to interpret incoming information in unique ways. Our perceptions determine if half a glass of water is "half-full" or "half-empty." Our perceptions can make a stressor a monster or a mouse, a bogeyman or a will-o-the-wisp. In other words, stress is "in the eye of the beholder."

So every time Org encounters the saber-toothed tiger, he is scared out of his cave-bear shorts and he comes to associate (conditioning, right?) all those autonomic responses (pounding heart, rapid breathing, tightness in the gut, etc.) with "fear." Similarly, when he is chased by the cave bear, the giant three-toed sloth, or his mother-in-law, it's the same association: autonomic arousal = **fear!** Then one day his grandma dies—his heart pounds, his breathing is rapid, his gut aches—but this **feels** different, so he calls it "sadness" or "depression!" Org has just discovered another important principle: The labeling of an emotion (e.g., fear vs. depression) starts with a **physiological state** that is **interpreted** based on what **past experience** has taught us about the **context**—got it?

> **Physiological state** is
> **interpreted,** based on
> **past experiences** within a certain
> **context**

The physiological state at Grandma's funeral = "sad"
The physiological state being chased by a bear = "fear"
The physiological state when food is being stolen = "anger" etc.

O.K. Org has **emotions** down cold, or so he thinks. Then one day he discovers that some physiological state can be kicked off by a Neanderthal double-shot latte, bungee jumping over cliffs, or a visit from the in-laws. Now Org is really confused. Can coffee or bungee jumping make him "afraid?" And how can just his in-laws coming to visit make him "fearful?"

Org has discovered that biology, cognitive behavior, and the environment are all **connected** (remember the "star" on page 12?) and that various combinations of these factors can give rise to emotions. He has also discovered that emotions can be confusing and can cloud our perceptions (e.g., "Am I having a heart attack or am I afraid?") And he has discovered that you can be afraid of things that haven't even happened yet.

The terms "fear" and "anxiety" are generally regarded as synonymous, although the classical distinction between fear and anxiety describes the former as referring to a specific danger, whereas the latter refers to anticipated, diffuse, and sometimes unknown danger. The object is known in fear; the object is unknown in anxiety.

Clinical Strategies For Stress Management

Which brings us back to your patients. When they enter your office, they may be anxious, anticipating unknown or vague danger as they confront a threatening disease. In the clinic, you can minimize this anxiety by providing your patient with accurate information. As a physician, providing **accurate information** in terms of **what** to expect, **when** to expect it, **how much** discomfort or pain to expect for **how long,** and **why** the procedure is being done can substantially reduce your patient's stress. Remember what we said about information being reinforcing? Realistic answers to a patient's questions serve to clarify perceptions and permit him to respond in a more adaptive manner. And when you provide such information in a friendly, supportive, and realistic manner, you are also reducing stress by becoming part of his support network. A double WAMI toward stress reduction! Org would be proud! (F-f-f-f-f-fantastic!)

What can be done about stress in your office practice? In addition to providing **accurate information** in an accepting and understanding manner, reality-based **reassurance** is helpful. Provide the patient some degree of **control,** be it over her pain, some facets of treatment, or just giving her something to do. Anything which increases your patient's perceived ability to influence what is or what will be happening to her will decrease her emotional arousal and stress level.

Several other **behavioral strategies** might also prove helpful in your stress management repertoire:

1) Relaxation training
2) Exercise
3) Proper nutrition
4) Guided imagery or creative visualization techniques
5) Hypnosis
6) Biofeedback training
7) Recreation

Keep in mind, however, that the two primary sources of stress reduction occur through **modification of one's perceptions** of the problem and one's ability to solve it and **social support.**

Sometimes fear is strong enough that an individual begins to avoid situations. And **avoidance leads to further avoidance** and **increased fears.** (Go back and read about "negative reinforcement" on page 15 and see if you can explain why.) When this occurs, we say the patient is engaging in **phobic avoidant behavior.** Now, if you understand how the avoidant behavior was learned, you know what we have to do to **un**learn it.

Exposure Therapy Demonstrated

As we discussed on page 14, one effective behavioral technique designed to reduce fears and avoidant behavior is exposure therapy.

Exposure therapy involves three steps:

1) Identifying fear-inducing situations
2) Arranging them in order from least to most fearful
3) Exposing oneself to each situation, one at a time, to reconstruct the fear-inducing cues and the fear itself. This last step can be done in a real life situation (*in vivo*) or can be imagined (*in vitro*).

Let's demonstrate how the process works. The patient is asked to imagine an anxiety-producing scene and to generate and tolerate the anxiety response for about a minute. Emotions are normal autonomic responses to certain situations.

The point is to allow them to occur, get familiar with them, and handle them (not run from them). Emotions are not "crazy." Our interpretations of them, however, do not always follow the laws of syllogistic reasoning. (Remember what we said about the "meaning" we assign to our behavior and our feelings?) If emotions are themselves "normal," then it is our **interpretations** of them that may need revising—especially in cases where fear is leading us to avoid situations. So let's return to our exposure therapy and see how these concepts help us revise interpretations of **fear.**

Remember stressed-out Dorothy, the air traffic control lady? We promised you that we would return to treat her. Let's assume she has become fearful of her job situation and has started avoiding it, calling in sick, etc. We might ask Dorothy to imagine several situations that cause her fear. We ask her to imagine increasingly complex situations on her air traffic control radar screen. Beginning with the least demanding, she imagines the scene and experiences the anxiety. At this point you might ask Dorothy to imagine herself **relaxing** on a feather bed in her farm house in Kansas, resting comfortably, letting her muscles grow heavy and relaxed, and feeling deeply that all is right with the world. By following the **anxiety-producing scene** with a **relaxation response,** the relaxation response will erode the anxiety response, thereby reducing fear. Such a process is called the **Principle of Reciprocal Inhibition.** That is, because you can't be anxious and relaxed at the same time, the relaxation response and the anxiety response cancel each other out, or reciprocally inhibit each other. In Dorothy's case, her image of being relaxed in Kansas interferes with and reduces her fear of airplane disasters on her shift. In the process she also learns to tolerate the anxiety and is less fearful of it, i.e., less afraid of fear.

Let's say you're pressed for time. Snow White and the Seven Dwarfs have been in your waiting room for two hours so you don't have time to get Dorothy relaxed by imagining herself lounging about in a feather bed in Kansas. Go to Plan B. Have Dorothy imagine her fearful scene: She's in the control tower, her relief is stuck in traffic, she's been at work all day and four planes are trying to land simultaneously—on three runways. She reports to you that, yes, the scene makes her feel *very* anxious. In fact, she is near panic. You ask her to focus on the fear—concentrate on it totally—study it thoroughly—keep concentrating on it, etc.

After one to two minutes Dorothy reports that the anxiety has peaked and (surprise!) is beginning to come down. This experience is known to anyone who has ever confronted fear in an avoidant situation—it peaks, then comes down. Why?

The parasympathetic nervous system works in opposition to the sympathetic, to keep body processes from going wacko when we are stressed. This is one of those homeostatic things—fear does *not* continue to escalate until we explode. There is a built in governor that shuts off the fear response and begins to reduce it.

By focusing on the fear, Dorothy **does not** engage in the avoidance response. She does not negatively reinforce the response to the fear. She allows the homeostatic function of the parasympathetic nervous system to do its work. She becomes familiar and more comfortable with her fear and she feels great because now she is **in control!**

As the story of Dorothy illustrates, the 21st-century saber-toothed tiger prowls in the jungle of our minds, assuming a variety of shapes and sizes, shifting its fearsome attack in the shadows of our consciousness. Prehistoric Org was lucky. All he needed to defeat his tiger was speed and a club.

SUMMARY AND KEY CONCEPTS

With his mouth full of mastodon while celebrating his victory over the tiger, Org summarizes several important stress issues: (1) **fight or flight response** and (2) alarm, resistance and exhaustion, the three components of Selye's **General Adaptation Syndrome.**

The two principal mediators of one's stress response are: (1) one's **perceptions** and (2) **social support.**

Solutions within a clinical environment to patient stress include:

1) Providing accurate **information:** what, when, how much, how long and why.
2) **Reassurance**
3) Providing patients some degree of **control.**

Behavioral strategies for stress management include:

1) Relaxation training
2) Exercise
3) Proper nutrition
4) Visualization/imagery techniques
5) Hypnosis
6) Biofeedback training
7) Recreation
8) Tiger trouncing and mastodon mastication (If it worked for Org, it might work for you!)

Exposure therapy can be as simple as "one, two, three" in treating avoidant and phobic behaviors effectively:

1) Identify the fear-inducing situations.
2) Arrange them in order from least to most fearful.
3) Expose the patient to each anxiety-producing situation.

Exposure therapy offers anxiety-burdened patients time away from their emotional caves and promotes less fear-driven lives.

CHAPTER 8

CHRONIC PAIN: WHEN THE MEDICINE CHEST FAILS

Pain is Personal

I'll not soon forget the fear and anger in her eyes, as my youngest daughter screamed in the doctor's office. She had just ripped her finger open, and I was holding her down on a gurney while the attending physician was injecting her with an anesthetic in preparation for stitches. She was hurting, but she was also frightened because she didn't know what was going to happen to her. Her pain had turned to suffering, and I hated it. This was my daughter and nothing was ever to harm her.

Years of clinical experience in pain management have confirmed what I learned from my daughter: Pain is a highly personal experience that runs much deeper into our souls than simple tissue trauma. But pain is not just a solo experience. Our pain spills over onto our families, onto those we love and who love us, and when the pain persists, when it becomes chronic, it changes our lives and theirs, too.

Eighty percent of the people you will see in your practice will be in some kind of pain. Unlike the preceding example, a good deal of their pain will have *no* current biological cause. Does that mean its just an "ouch that needs a couch" (i.e., pain "in the patient's head" that should be dealt with by a psychiatrist)? Nope. There is no such thing as "imaginary pain." Think about it. Who in the world would want to suffer ongoing, long-term pain?! Nobody is that crazy.

You are going to be in the front lines combating pain so you will need to know a great deal more about such issues as acute vs. chronic pain, biomedical models vs. learning models for treating pain, and levels of pain perception. However, there are no easy definitions and no definitive explanations of pain, and its meaning can be highly subjective. Therefore, how **you** and **your patient** define pain will determine how you treat it.

Medical science still flounders somewhat about the concept and meaning of pain. Our current thinking about pain stems from ancient roots, borrowing from the philosophy of Aristotle and later from Rene Descartes, both of whom viewed pain as a physical process: A patient's response to pain is directly related to the sensory stimulus. That is, burning one's finger on the stove causes one's pain.

Acute vs. Chronic Pain

In general, there are two types of pain: acute and chronic. **Acute** pain refers to tissue damage (i.e., nociceptive input), generally does not require long-term adaptation or relearning in order to adjust to it, and can be treated aggressively by medication. **Chronic** pain, in contrast, frequently does not involve readily definable tissue damage, can actually be made worse by pain-killing medications, is demonstrated over a long period of time and requires major adjustment and life changes to compensate for it. As a rule of thumb in medical practice, what is prescribed for acute pain management is contraindicated for chronic pain management.

Biomedical and Learning Models of Pain

Recognition of these two types of pain yield two models of pain management: (1) the biomedical model and (2) the learning/operant model. In the **biomedical model,** a patient's symptoms are considered a function of underlying tissue pathology or nociceptive input. This model is useful in treating acute problems of recent onset or time-limited pain. It has, however, diminishing effectiveness in treating chronic pain. As a general rule, the longer a pain problem lasts (e.g., six months or longer), the less likely the biomedical model will have clinical usefulness. With the passage of time, acute pain causes changes in patient behavior and these "pain behaviors" cause others to respond differently to the patient. As we saw earlier, these "consequences" can have a rewarding effect on the "pain behaviors," reinforcing them, sustaining them—in effect causing them to become chronic. Unfortunately, when pain becomes more chronic, and therefore more likely to be impacted by learning and the surrounding environment, an alternative model for viewing pain may be necessary. However, our health care system operates under the biomedical model; it only provides care for biologic causes (i.e., tissue damage, nociceptive pain).

Figure 8-1:   Biomedical Model of Pain

The **learning/operant model,** in contrast, is derived from research that shows that pain behavior, when chronic, will be controlled predominantly by its consequences. For example, chronic pain may be rewarded and thereby maintained if it results in the patient's avoiding adverse consequences. Chronic pain may also be maintained by a patient receiving rewards for displaying pain behavior, rewards that can include:

1) **Attention** from relatives and nurses
2) **Rest** and relief from work or family obligations
3) **Medication** that relieves pain
4) **Disability compensation** and other financial rewards

In managing chronic pain, it should be emphasized that the biomedical model is not discarded, but that the learning model perspective must be incorporated to address the unique demands that conditioning plays in the development of chronic pain.

Hiding under such academic distinctions, however, is a bias which can alter your demeanor as a healer. After pain treatment proves ineffective, and the patient continues to cry out for relief, it is highly seductive to brand him as an hysteric, "whiner," malingerer, a "hypochondriac," or less elegantly, a "crock." Such statements as "he must really enjoy being sick" are unfortunately all too frequently heard during coffee breaks in clinical settings. Understandably, one grows weary in treating sick people, particularly the ones who don't get better. Healing can be a frustrating profession, and we sometimes say things out of frustration we don't literally mean. But no patients, no matter what their secondary gain or compensation status may be, want to hurt and continue to grapple with pain. The critical point to be made is that in the care of protracted chronic pain, it is the treatment, not the patient, that has failed. More specifically, it is likely that the misapplication of acute pain (biomedical) treatments to chronic pain (learning/operant) problems has produced poor results. When we come up short, it's time to go back to the drawing board and develop a more viable paradigm.

The Loeser Model of Pain Levels

Pain and what it means represent highly complex and largely misunderstood phenomena. Perhaps the most lucid and helpful model to date is a conceptualization of pain by Dr. John Loeser, a neurosurgeon from the University of Washington School of Medicine. He postulates a four-tiered model of pain.

NOCICEPTION
PAIN
SUFFERING
PAIN BEHAVIOR

Figure 8-2: Loeser Pain Model

1) **Nociception,** or **tissue damage,** refers to "potentially tissue-damaging thermal or mechanical energy impinging upon specialized nerve endings of A Delta and C fibers." When you step on a tack with your bare feet, you experience nociception/tissue damage at the point the tack enters your foot.

2) **Pain** refers to your **perceptions** of tissue damage. If you are walking down a mountain trail in your bare feet, are confronted by a Grizzly, and then step on a tack, you probably wouldn't perceive pain until you were well beyond the clutches of the bear. Nociceptive injury does not necessarily produce pain perception. There is no one-to-one relationship between tissue damage and pain perception.

3) **Suffering** refers to a negative emotional response to perceived tissue injury. If someone slams your chest with a forearm smash, you experience a trauma (nociception), feel the blow (pain), and have a negative emotional reaction such as anger, hurt, etc. However, if you were a member of a football team and received such a block, the coach might congratulate you for a job well done. You would have been hit, felt the blow, but **not** suffered. Rather, you would be feeling great because of the coach's praise and the fine job of blocking.

4) **Pain behavior,** the only part of this process which is directly observable, is activity which reflects the presence of negative emotional responses to perceptions of tissue damage (e.g., complaints, grimacing, taking medication, refusing to work, etc.). Pain behavior, like any behavior, is influenced by its consequences (i.e., can be conditioned). Put more simply, **pain behavior is learned.**

Treatment of Chronic Pain

If indeed there is a significant learned component involved with chronic pain, then treatment intervention should be planned accordingly. In terms of chronic pain, such intervention frequently includes:

1) Reduce and/or eliminate all **pain medication.** As we have already seen, medication administered on a PRN (as you need it) basis can actually increase pain complaints if the drugs are made pain contingent, i.e., given whenever the patient experiences pain. A vicious conditioning/addiction cycle can be set into motion, with more pain signaling more medication, and the relief provided by the medication **negatively reinforcing** more pain . . . and more medication! Thus, patients' pain meds should be put on a **time-contingent,** not pain contingent (PRN) basis, and then gradually reduced. Occasionally, it may become necessary to hospitalize a patient for detoxification purposes. In this controlled environment, the patient's drug usage is evaluated, then gradually eliminated by reducing the active chemical ingredients in a cherry syrup "pain cocktail" by 10% each day for ten days. If a patient is then placed on further medication, it is impor-

tant to insure that the prescription is **time contingent,** i.e., taken at a certain time each day.

2) Increase the patient's **activity level.** Such activity expansion may include physical therapy, recreational activities with family and friends, and a gradual return to some level of work, etc. When physical activity is involved, the therapeutic concept of **working to quota** is important. After determining an exercise baseline (e.g., five sit-ups a session), the patient is then required to start slightly below this baseline and exercise each day until he reaches this target or quota, rather than stopping when he feels pain (i.e., **working to tolerance**). The quota is then raised gradually. Working only to tolerance keeps a patient a slave to his "pain bell" (i.e., when pain occurs, activity stops). In contrast, working to quota shapes him to higher levels of physical performance (and less pain).

3) Reduce **acute pain treatment.** As indicated earlier, treatment for chronic benign pain is generally the opposite of treatment prescribed for acute pain. But doctors hate to see people in pain, so when more conservative treatments do not work, they consider more aggressive acute pain approaches. As we have seen, not only do these acute pain treatments not work, but they can actually contribute to the chronic pain problem. Thus, at some point, the cures may become worse than the disease.

4) Restructure the patient's **perceptions** of pain, the bases for these perceptions, and the meaning his pain has for him. How do these perceptions influence his behavior and the behavior of those around him? Does his behavior help or contribute to the chronic pain problem? Pain does not occur in a vacuum. Recall Chapter 6 on Medical Care and the Family: It's important to examine the interpersonal and the intrapersonal underpinnings of a patient's pain problems.

5) Teach the patient how to rally and use his **support system,** particularly immediate family and friends. Chronic pain has a ripple effect, touching the lives of those around the patient, and, tragically, pushing many of them away.

6) Be alert to the presence of secondary emotional reactions such as **anxiety** and **depression.** In fact, in the case of chronic pain, one can safely assume the presence of depression in response to long-term, unsuccessful treatment of pain (unless proven otherwise).

It's been years now since my daughter's finger, temper, and pain challenged the emergency room doctor. I have not grown to love pain anymore than I did then, but I have become a respecter of this complex phenomena and more appreciative of the array of factors that contribute to its occurrence and treatment.

SUMMARY AND KEY CONCEPTS

Pain will be your regular clinical companion. Knowledge of several concepts will make your journey together easier.

1) **Acute vs. Chronic Pain**
2) **Biomedical vs. Learning/Operant Model**
3) **Levels of Pain**
    a) Nociception
    b) Pain
    c) Suffering
    d) Pain Behavior

Intervention strategies for treating chronic pain with behavioral management techniques include the following directives:

1) Reduce and/or eliminate all pain **medication.**
2) Increase patient's **activity** level.
3) Decrease acute **health care use.**
4) Explore and restructure the patient's **perceptions** of her pain.
5) Enable and enhance the patient's **support system.**
6) Rule out secondary **depression** and **anxiety.**

CHAPTER 9

DEPRESSION: A CAR WITHOUT GAS AND NOWHERE TO GO

Every day in your medical practice you will see at least one depressed patient. That is a promise. Every day! How you deal with these patients will determine your emotional survival as well as theirs. A wise little known Western psychologist once described the primary characteristic of depression as "energy-draining," not only for the patient but also for those around him. Depression is tragically ironic: Depressed folks hunger for emotional strokes from others, but depression may come between them. Other people can avoid them like the plague, fearing that depression has turned them into emotional leeches. A patient, or even a close friend or family member can seem like an emotional bottomless pit, needing more and more reassurance and support, giving little personally in return, but coming back for more and more emotional energy. Picture yourself in a busy medical practice, well behind in seeing your scheduled patients. Dan the Depressed stares at you as you enter the examining room. Chances are there will be two people depressed by the end of the appointment: Dan, the energy drainer, and guess who?

It is estimated that several million people in the U.S. require treatment for depression each year, a number that far surpasses the resources available from psychiatric specialists. Therefore, the majority of depressed patients first seek their personal physician for relief. That could be you! Most of these patients will present medical complaints that are symptomatic of depression or complicated or aggravated by their depression. The lifetime risk for becoming clinically depressed is 8 to 12 % for men and 20 to 26 % for women. Depression with a capital *D* has become a major public health concern. It is the cause of loss of intrapersonal and interpersonal effectiveness, loss of work hours and productivity, and significant personal cost to family and friends. In addition, suicidal thinking, suicide attempts, and suicide itself are distressingly common with the depressed: In fact, people with depressive illness kill themselves at approximately ten times the frequency of patients with other psychiatric diagnoses.

Some patients who suffer from depression experience it as primarily an emotional and psychological problem, and they talk about it in those terms. However, the family doctor will often see patients with depression who present with a physical complaint. Often these patients will either present amplified medical problems or will have symptoms of undetermined cause. Your first impulse will be to treat these "medical complaints." But unless you recognize their origin and treat their cause, you will become as frustrated and depressed as your patient! In my work at the Denver Veterans Administration Hospital, for example, the vast majority of depressed patients spoke of their suffering not in psychological terms (i.e., "I feel hopeless, helpless or worthless") but in terms of physical symptoms (i.e., "I can't sleep, food tastes awful, I don't have any appetite, my lower back is hurting more, my gut still aches, etc."). This chapter provides a framework for a diagnostic interview, reviews the most important differential diagnostic points, looks at the etiology including developing biological correlates of depression, and reviews the currently available treatment methods.

Diagnosis of Depression

"I think I got the reverse 'Midas touch' Doc," one depressed patient once muttered. "Everything I touch seems to turn to crap!" This poignant comment reflects the state of mind knows as **dysphoria** which, when persistent, is a primary ingredient of depression. It is a prolonged and pervasive emotional state for which patients use a number of descriptive words: depressed, sad, blue, hopeless, bored, gloomy, dejected.

Some depressed patients will deny that they are depressed but, instead, will acknowledge **anhedonia,** the loss of one's ability to experience pleasure. The bloom they feel is off the rose. If a person won the lottery, he would probably complain because now he has to pay more taxes.

Depressed patients report deflated self-esteem along with bruised and negative **self concepts.** They describe themselves as hopeless and worthless, and they feel helpless about improving their lot in life. They have negative thoughts not only about themselves, but also about the world and the future. They are often in a state of giving up, feeling that nothing they do seems to make any difference anyway. This condition, called **learned helplessness,** is the result of a seemingly lifelong history of minimal rewards and satisfaction . . . a life of extinction trials!

Accompanying dysphoria up to 50% of the time is the psychic nemesis, **anxiety,** which can serve to agitate and rattle the saber of fear. Occasionally, anxiety can actually mask an underlying depression, as anxiety symptoms generally are more compelling and obvious. Like the proverbial "squeaky wheel," one's fears and anxieties may make more racket than the subtler quiet hell of depression. **Anger** may also accompany depression, especially in patients who alternate between expressing their frustrations outwardly (e.g., in work and interpersonal relationships) and periodically blaming themselves.

While the emotional aspects of depression are important, it is necessary for the clinician to realize that depressive illness is more than just an emotional state. To diagnose every patient who is sad and gloomy as depressed, especially when somatic therapies are being considered, is a mistake. A patient's sad emotional reactions are often appropriate temporary responses to stressful life events. These reactions, which we might label as depression with a small *d,* deserve your attention too, but rarely require extensive psychotherapy, medication, or more aggressive medical treatment.

By contrast, depressive illness (that's depression with a capital *D*), is a more complex syndrome. In addition to emotional disturbances, depressed patients have cognitive, behavioral, physiological, and sometimes perceptual problems. A proper diagnosis requires an evaluation of each of these areas.

Diagnostic Criteria for Depression

Criteria established by the American Psychiatric Association for the diagnosis of Depression include the following:

1) Depressed mood—sad, blue, "down"
2) Anhedonia—Markedly diminished interest or pleasure in activities
3) Vegetative signs, including:
   a) Significant change in weight and/or appetite
   b) Sleep disturbance (insomnia or hypersomnia)
4) Psychomotor agitation or retardation
5) Fatigue or loss of energy
6) Feelings of worthless or guilt
7) Poor concentration or difficulty making decisions
8) Suicidal ideation

If five of the above symptoms are present for a two-week period, including dysphoria and/or anhedonia, diagnose depression.

Treatments of Depression

For the majority of the patients that you will see in a general office practice, short-term counseling or psychotherapy will prove to be more than sufficient for remedying their depression. The passage of time, the resolution of immediate life stresses, and spontaneous remission of depression appear to be three active factors accounting for most people recovering from depression. The only good thing about depression is that it does end.

In brief psychotherapy for the treatment of depression, the focus is typically on the patient's **immediate stresses** or problems. The failure to resolve life problems is a frequent cause of depression. In the vast majority of circumstances, you will be able to determine what problems in your patient's life are triggering or contributing to the depression. Once you have identified these problems you will be able to embark, with the patient, on strategies designed to reduce or resolve these stresses. Do not make the mistake, however, of simply being a problem solver of the patient's woes. Your task is to assist the patient in solving his own problems. It's imperative that you first establish an empathic relationship in which the patient feels understood, accepted, and respected. Once the patient feels that you have "walked in his shoes," then you may offer solicited advice and training in problem-solving skills.

Many times it is not so much a matter of the depressed patient needing advice as much as getting some emotional energy. One metaphor that is helpful for us is conceptualizing depression as being "out of gas". Patients can be like a car with an empty gas tank. The gas tank has been depleted primarily by repeated failures, frustration, negative perceptions, low self-esteem, worry . . . all contributing to a lack of sleep and overextending the amount of energy reserve.

Within this perspective, your focus can be threefold:

1) Getting the patient energized
2) Helping your patient decide where he wants to go
3) Clarifying how he wants to get there. Sounds like a psychological AAA: fueling up, targeting a destination, and selecting a road map to get him there!

Obviously, before a person can worry about where to drive a car, he has to have some gas in the tank, i.e., energy. Providing such energy by means of medication, stress reduction, and supportive counseling are the primary "gas stations" or intervention strategies available to you.

Cognitive Behavior Therapy (CBT) has been shown to be a highly effective psychotherapy modality. Within this psychotherapeutic model the following characteristics are associated with clinical improvement in depression:

1) Realistic **reassurance**
2) A supportive, **caring attitude**
3) The enlistment of friends and family to **support** the patient
4) The challenging of negative and self defeating beliefs
5) Medication management when necessary

The preceding factors represent the most effective combination of intervention strategies.

With most depressed patients, **misconceptions** or distorted cognitions about themselves and their condition run rampant. Patients may feel that they are in a

hopeless situation and **helpless** to do anything about their condition, may **fear** that they will be cursed forever by depression, may worry that they will **never improve,** and may panic at the thought of "**losing their minds.**"

One important strategy in dealing with depression is to **predict** for patients what type of clinical course they can expect. For example, they can expect **fear** or apprehensiveness to fill their lives, they may experience some immediate **memory** problems and problems in **concentration.** They may suffer from **insomnia** and early morning awakening. Their **tempers** may be short, and they can many times experience unaccountable irritation. There may be a **loss of libido** or sexual interest. Some may experience **suicidal thoughts,** but **thinking** suicidal thoughts is not unexpected, and is quite different from **acting** on them. Finally, patients should be advised that they will be on an emotional **roller coaster** for awhile. Quite naturally, they will experience ups and downs, but these peaks and valleys are by no means signs of bad news or evidence that their condition is worsening.

After sketching some of the possible symptoms encountered in the clinical course of depression, it is helpful to discuss the benefits and potential responses to antidepressant medication, including common side effects. Traditionally, the drug treatment of depression has involved three general classes of drugs: (1) **Heterocyclic antidepressants (HCAs); (2) Monoamine Oxidase Inhibitors (MAO's);** and (3) **Lithium** salts. From such medications, many patients can expect dry mouths, blurred vision, and some feelings of drowsiness the first several days on medication (to mention only some of the potential side effects). They should also be aware that it takes several days, sometimes a week to ten days, before they experience any antidepressant impact from the medication itself. With improved sleep the first day or two, however, they can begin to feel renewed energy, the vanguard of better things ahead!

Knowing these symptoms and being able to identify and recognize them as **natural** symptoms of depression (not evidence that they are "going crazy") can be most reassuring to depressed patients, who are already feeling their share of vulnerability!

SUMMARY AND KEY CONCEPTS

In your routine clinical work, be aware of these **warning signs of depression:**

1) Dysphoria
2) Anhedonia
3) Negative self concept
4) Anxiety
5) Anger

The generally accepted **diagnostic criteria** for clinical depression include the following characteristics:

1) Depressed mood
2) Anhedonia
3) Vegetative changes
   a) Significant change in weight and/or appetite
   b) Sleep disturbance
4) Agitation or motor retardation
5) Loss of energy
6) Feelings of guilt and worthlessness
7) Problems in concentration
8) Difficulty making decisions
9) Suicidal thinking

The clinical **treatment for depression** (i.e., managing your patient's empty gas tank), might well include the following strategies:

1) Identification and intervention into **stressors**
2) Supportive **counseling**
   a) Cognitive Behavior Therapy
   b) Discussing and clarifying misconceptions
   c) Predicting clinical course
3) **Medication,** when necessary, which typically involves:
   a) HCAs
   b) MAOs
   c) Lithium

CHAPTER 10

SUICIDE: "OH GOD, IS THERE NO ONE TO LISTEN?"

Centuries before modern medicine, the Roman philosopher Seneca gave eloquent voice to the despair and utter estrangement of the tormented soul:

> Behold me in my nakedness, my wounds, my secret
> Grief, my despair, my betrayal, my pain,
> My tongue which cannot express my sorrow, my
> Terror, my abandonment.
>
> Listen to me for a day—an hour—a moment!
> Lest I expire in my terrible wilderness, my
> Lonely silence. O God, is there no one to listen?

And what happens when there is no one—no one to listen, to comfort, to console. There can be the longing and searching for death. There can be the risk of suicide.

Risk Factors in Suicide

The acronym **SAD PERSONS** helps to identify ten major **risk factors** for suicide:

Sex (Males are at greater risk than females for killing themselves, although females threaten suicide at a higher rate.)
Age (Persons over forty)
Depression

Previous attempts
Ethanol abuse (Alcohol fans the flames of self destruction.)
Recent loss of an important relationship
Social support lacking
Organized plan by the patient for self-destruction
No spouse (Single persons statistically are at greater risk.)
Sickness (Serious illness increases the incidence of suicide.)

The incidence of suicidal deaths in our country is indeed sobering. Suicide is the tenth leading cause of death in the U.S., the second leading cause of death on college campuses, and the leading cause of death among medical students. There are 25,000 suicides in the U.S. each year with ten times that number attempting suicide.

"So what has this got to do with me?" you ask. Eighty percent of those who killed themselves saw their physicians within six months before their death. Fifty percent saw their doctors within one month before they killed themselves. Got your attention yet? How about this: Twenty percent died from prescriptions from their doctors. Fifty percent had obtained the means to kill themselves in a single prescription from their doctors. These tragic data clearly underline the double edged sword—the drug that heals can also slay.

So what would be helpful to know about suicide? First, let's dispel some myths about suicide:

MYTH	FACT
People who talk about suicide won't try it.	They talk and some die.
Suicidal individuals are fully intent on dying and do not want to be rescued.	In weighing the pros's and con's, the patient generally casts a close, split vote to die.
Asking about suicide may put a dangerous idea into the patient's head.	With depression, one should assume that suicidal ideation is already present unless proven otherwise.
Suicidal people are suicidal forever.	Time delay has saved lives.
People who try suicide and fail are not serious about it, and will not try again.	Previous attempts are red flags for high suicidal risk.
Only crazy people commit suicide	People in pain commit suicide.

Figure 10-1: Myths and Facts about Suicide

Suicidal Clues

Fortunately, before patients decide to kill themselves, they frequently provide **clues** that can tip off the physician and others that this person is at risk. In general, such clues can be classified in terms of four broad types: verbal, behavioral, situational and syndromatic.

1) **Verbal:** Direct statements such as, "I want to kill myself." Indirect statements include comments which mirror the person's intolerable existence: "You're better off without me." In such indirect communications, it's necessary to put in effort to "read between the lines."

2) **Behavioral:** Actions such as a "practice run," an actual suicide attempt, or other "cries for help." Don't try to "second guess" a suicide threat. A lot of time is wasted trying to determine if a person "really means it" or not. **Take the person at his word! Believe, and act accordingly!** Indirect behavioral indicators include putting one's personal affairs in order, giving away prized possessions, and basically acting as if one is wrapping up one's life.

3) **Situational:** Perceived crises create chaos. A manageable disease can become a monstrous illness in the eye of the ailing patient, who can feel backed into an "incurable" corner with no hope of escape. Ironically, many terminal patients do not feel suicidal, although one cardinal risk factor for suicide is deteriorating health. As a physician, it is imperative that you understand your patient's view of his condition, the perceptual "spin" that he may give medical information about himself, and the extent to which he has interpreted such information as boding bad news and hopeless prospects. Although we may generally agree that certain situations may be traumatic events, and we nod in agreement that "he ought to feel suicidal" in the face of such adversity, we still need to view such events through the eye of the beholder. We need to see if the patient sees his glass as half full or half empty. We must not confuse **our** view of the situation with that of the patient.

   The renowned Viennese psychoanalyst Viktor Frankl once made the observation that while interred in a Nazi concentration camp, he would see men entering the camp in generally the same condition. They were exposed in similar degrees to the harsh weather, guard brutality, poor nutrition, and general abuse. But upon liberation, some left battered and beaten while others seemed almost the better for having gone through such trials. Your best assurance in understanding your patient's intent is to be as familiar with his belief about his condition, his life circumstances, and his future prognosis (as conjectural as it can sometimes be).

4) **Syndromatic:** Dr. Edwin Shneidman, a leading American psychologist, former Director of the L.A. Suicide Prevention Center, and leading researcher in the area of suicidology, postulates four clusters of suicidal symptoms:

a) **Depression:** There is a shifting of a person's psychological interests from the interpersonal to the intrapersonal crisis within himself. Willingness to communicate is compromised. Detachment and withdrawal from life are common. In such cases, first aid in suicide prevention is directed at counteracting the person's feelings of hopelessness by transmitting personal support with a firm and hopeful attitude. Such support helps the patient view reality more clearly and through less dark-colored glasses.

b) **Disorientation:** Suicidal risk is escalated when a patient's perceptions become distorted by delusions or hallucinations. Such a person's behavior is a challenge to predict. Destructive behavior may be triggered by a crazed thought, a hallucinated command, a fleeting intense fear within a delusional system, or a brain muddled from toxic chemicals.

c) **Hopeless defiance:** Some patients, no matter how painful their lives, attempt to retain some shred of control over their fate. Thus a man dying of cancer may, rather than passively giving into his disease, choose to "call his last shot" and play one last active role in his own life by picking the time of his death.

d) **Dissatisfied dependence:** The patient may begin to feel frustrated and a failure because no matter what he does, there seem to be no options remaining.

This psychological "dead end" can result in simultaneous feelings of increasing dependence and dissatisfaction with this dependence. For example, an inpatient becomes more dependent upon his caregivers but increasingly dissatisfied with his care. Feelings of inadequacy and guilt can build, as he makes more demands and displays a greater need for attention and reassurance. Thus, the "Tyranny of Dependency" can be a double-edged sword that turns inward on its wielder.

Suicide Prevention Strategies

The Los Angeles Suicide Prevention Center offers five steps for preventing suicide:

1) Establish a **relationship,** maintain psychological **contact,** and obtain **information** from the patient. **Listen** nonjudgmentally. **Reassure** the person of your interest, concern and availability for help.

2) Most important, **identify** and **clarify** the focal problem. **What is so bad that suicide seems the only alternative?** If we can help the patient find a solution to this problem, the need for suicide disappears! Most suicidal patients are confused, disorganized, and flooded with feeling. They suffer from perceptual tunnel vision: They can't view the big picture, being unable to see the forest for the trees.

3) **Assess suicide potential.** Consider such variables as the patient's age, sex, psychological symptoms, stress level, presence of a concrete suicide plan,

history of prior suicide attempts, current medical status, and the status of key relationships and his ability to communicate with them.

4) Evaluate the patient's strengths and **resources** for resolving the focal problems.

5) Develop a constructive **intervention partnership** and **plan.** Obtain the patient's commitment to this plan of action (in writing, if possible, as many people fear lawyers suing them for breach of contract—even when they are suicidal!), and mobilize the patient's own resources as well as the resources of others in response to him.

In reviewing all of this information, you, as a physician, are capable of developing strategies for suicide prevention. You can be a lifesaver, a one-person "congress" who can help shift the patient's votes from the death side of the aisle to the side of life. To paraphrase Dr. Shneidman, doctors do not need elaborate pieces of mechanical equipment; all they require are sharp eyes and ears, good intuition, a pinch of wisdom, some common sense, an ability to act appropriately, and a deep resolve to make a positive difference in a troubled patient's life.

SUMMARY AND KEY CONCEPTS

Few clinical cluster of symptoms challenges a doctor's diagnostic skills like a suicidal patient. The acronym SAD PERSON can help you keep some of the **risk factors** in mind.

Many **myths** surround suicide, some of which can be impediments to effective intervention and treatment.

Clues for suicide often can be found in the following areas:

1) Verbal
2) Behavioral
3) Situational
4) Syndromatic clusters of suicidal characteristics:
   a) Depression
   b) Disorientation
   c) Hopeless defiance
   d) Dissatisfied dependence

Steps for suicide prevention involve the following steps:

1) Establish a supportive relationship—listen and reassure
2) Identify the problem
3) Assess suicide potential
4) Evaluate strengths
5) Develop an intervention partnership and plan

Remember, the vast majority of suicidal patients are in conflict about whether to live or die. You can be a significant factor in their decision.

CHAPTER 11

ALCOHOL ABUSE: THE POWER OF POISON

Not long ago a cartoon was published showing a disheveled man, obviously intoxicated, stumbling into his house late at night and being confronted by an angry wife with a rolling pin. The caption read, "Damn it, woman! I don't criticize you about your diseases, so don't yell at me about mine!" In times past, alcohol abuse has been variously considered a moral defect, a cozy relationship with the Roman god Bacchus, a sign of virility, and a 20th-century disease that cries out for treatment rather than punishment. Our society flirts with recognizing alcoholism as a major health care problem. Yet the best ads on Super Bowl Sunday are the beer commercials! Somebody must be buying the stuff! And just to bring the message a little closer to home, what do **you** plan to do to celebrate the end of some of your exams? Tip a few? Did we just hear you say under your breath, "Damn it, Seitz! I don't tease you about being a workaholic, so don't yell at me about unwinding in medical school"!

In spite of the media coverage allotted to drugs such as cocaine and heroin, dependence upon alcohol poses a much more substantial hazard to the collective public health. Approximately 100 million Americans drink alcoholic beverages, and between five and ten million of these drinkers are dependent upon this drug to an abusive degree.

Alcoholism Defined and Described

Alcoholism is a state in which alcohol means more to a person than the problems it causes. Thus, from a pragmatic medical viewpoint, a meaningful definition of alcoholism focuses on a person's alcohol consumption interfering significantly with work, family life, and ability to function effectively.

Whatever your definition of alcoholism, the abuse of the "nectar of the gods" cuts across all classes (including the whole gambit of educational experience and all socioeconomic classes) and all vocational groups. It is estimated that one out of every ten drinkers is a problem drinker or alcoholic. It is rare that any family in our culture does not contain problem drinkers. We all seem to have our "Uncle Jim" or "Grandpa Ralph," lovable rogues who urinate with high octane in the family punch bowl just before Father Mike blesses the Christmas goose. Their murder is instantly plotted by all present, but rarely executed. There are more often the ugly moments when venom flows from the bottle through her lips, as a mother curses her child for spilling milk on the kitchen floor. The toxic impact of a pickled punch from a drunken husband, a sarcastic slam-dunk sneer from an intoxicated loved one, the vacuous gaze of family "not all there" who have already been transported to "la la land" by booze. . . . Drinking is not exactly like the movies which feature a suave James Bond ordering his martini "shaken, not stirred." More than martinis are shaken by the effects of alcohol.

We all are familiar with a litany of disasters associated with alcohol abuse, but perhaps of more interest to the medical profession is the question of why persons with alcohol problems—or any other drug problem for that matter—continue to abuse their drug of choice. The answer is not a simple one. Many search for the immediate positive effect of alcohol—that "lift" or "boost," and then, later, a "mellow" feeling in which everyone is one's friend and the world is your personal oyster. Others use alcohol to "self-medicate," i.e., salve the hurt or pain inside, dilute the anxiety or worry, or jog their depression out of focus. These patterns are easy to slip into, as booze is its own reward (at least in the short haul) and can remove drinkers from aversive situations, both inside and outside their heads. (Now you understand the reasons for reading about positive and negative reinforcers!) And when the going gets tough . . . when alcohol means more to a person than the problems it causes . . . defense mechanisms like denial can flex their psychological muscles. An alcoholic can engage in massive denial that his or her drinking poses a social, occupational, or health hazard. Denial can be so robust that the affected individual can continue to abuse a drug such as alcohol for years before finally seeking help. Marriages can crumble, families can be torn apart, jobs can collapse, finances can disintegrate, health can be hobbled, and still the drinker or user can persist in his deadly dance with drugs for decades. (Don't let our alliteration drive you to drink!) It is not surprising, then, that hospital admissions for alcoholism peak during ages 45 through 54, even though alcohol abuse and dependence often begin in adolescence or early adulthood. During this middle-age period, not only do our bodies require more careful "care and feeding," but the infamous "midlife crises," major life changes (I'll talk about these later), and gosh knows what else provide ample temptation for "just one more drink."

Many alcohol abusers do not have the slightest idea that their drinking represents a pattern of dependence. It is as if every drinker's conception of "alcoholic" is "someone who drinks twice as much as I do." For this reason, merely asking a patient if he has an alcohol problem is unlikely to yield useful or accurate information. Instead, it is better to examine his drinking history, with emphasis on the following: gulping drinks, morning drinking, morning tremor, defensiveness about drinking, positive family history, blackouts, and problems alcohol creates with relationships at home and at work.

Evaluating Alcoholism

A number of brief but effective tests can be used in your office practice to gauge the extent of alcohol dependence, including the CAGE Questionnaire (*American Journal of Psychiatry,* 1974, **131:**1121):

1) Have you ever felt the need to **C**ut down on your drinking?
2) Have you ever felt **A**nnoyed by criticism of your drinking?
3) Have you had **G**uilt feelings about drinking?
4) Do you ever take a morning **E**ye-opener?

The short form of the Michigan Alcoholism Screening Test—MAST (*American Journal of Psychiatry,* 1971, **127**:1653) also provides an efficient office screening tool for alcohol problems:

		YES	NO
1)	Do you feel you're a normal drinker?	0	2
2)	Do friends or relatives think you are a normal drinker?	0	2
3)	Have you ever attended a meeting of Alcoholics Anonymous?	5	0
4)	Have you ever lost friends or girlfriends or boyfriends because of drinking?	2	0
5)	Have you ever gotten into trouble at work because of drinking?	2	0
6)	Have you ever neglected your obligations, your family, or your work for 2 or more days in a row because you were drinking?	2	0
7)	Have you ever had D.T.'s or severe shaking, heard voices, or seen things that weren't there after heavy drinking?	2	0
8)	Have you ever gone to anyone for help about your drinking?	5	0
9)	Have you ever been in a hospital because of drinking?	5	0
10)	Have you ever been arrested for drunk driving or driving after drinking?	2	0

[A score of 6 or more indicates problems with alcohol consumption]

Alcohol Impact on Body Systems

Following the diagnosis of alcohol problems, patients (and their doctors, too) need to be apprised of the unqualified havoc alcohol creates within the body:

1) **Cardiovascular system:** arrhythmias, premature ventricular contractions, hypertension
2) **Gastrointestinal system:** diarrhea, peptic ulcers, esophagitis, pancreatitis, poor teeth
3) **Neurological system:** "morning-after shakes," blackouts, amnesia, nystagmus, diffuse organic brain syndromes with impaired immediate memory and judgment, seizures
4) **Dermatology system:** jaundice, spider angiomata, "mahogany fingers" due to excessive smoking or cigarette burns, "table top" bruises from stumbling or falling, burns on arms from accidents
5) **Orthopedic system:** fractures, muscle wasting in the upper limbs and legs, Dupuytren's contractures (curling of small finger and third finger), aseptic necrosis of the femur
6) **Every organ system is poisoned by alcohol.** Anemia, low white count, elevated cholesterol, increased triglycerides, muscle aches, elevated uric acid, central nervous system changes. The list goes on and on and on.

The Clinical Course of Alcoholism

Some basic comments can be made about the course and natural history of alcoholism.

1) **The alcoholic can be unduly reassured by episodic and periodic sobriety.** However, it is sobriety which eventually is punctuated by falling off the wagon and increased drinking. Dr. James Smith, former Medical Director of the Schick Shadels Clinic in Seattle, makes the observation that one definitive test of a **non**alcoholic is to be able to take one drink daily (no more, no less) for thirty days. Alcoholics as well as nonalcoholics can abstain for thirty days, but alcoholics can't stop at one drink a day for thirty days. For an alcoholic, the booze determines the frequency of drinking, not the boozer.
2) **One third of alcoholics seem to quit on their own without any treatment.** They exhibit the characteristics of spontaneous remission. Why? It's not clear. Let's speculate. Are they able to do what other alcoholics can't, i.e., recognize the long-term consequences of their behaviors as more negative than the immediate rewards of inebriation?
3) **Alcoholics seem to respond to nonspecific intervention.** That is, to date at least, no precise treatment modes seem to do better in terms of helping alcoholics than more general and generic treatments such as group therapy, Alcoholics Anonymous, and straightforward discussion groups. There ap-

pears to be some immediate value in an Alcoholic Intervention (i.e., mediated confrontation by family and friends with specific examples of the patient's problems created by drinking) in getting the patient into immediate inpatient treatment. At this point, there does not appear to be any focused type of psychotherapy or medication that directly impacts alcoholism specifically or any compelling evidence for an "Alcoholic Personality."

Treatment of Alcoholism

In discussing the inpatient treatment of alcoholism, the primary rule of thumb to keep in mind is "Do no harm." Although the treatment of alcoholism may be general, the treatment for alcoholic withdrawal is quite specific. First of all, the alcohol withdrawal syndrome is a physiological reaction. This withdrawal syndrome can present a very severe type of physiological withdrawal process, although not always accompanied by D.T.'s (Delirium Tremens). Treatment should begin before the onset of such central nervous system changes as confusion, disorientation, and hallucinations. One of the earliest symptoms of D.T. withdrawal typically involves hand tremors. In terms of Delirium Tremens onset, the majority of symptoms will occur between six to twelve hours after the alcohol blood level has dropped below the usual level in the patient. D.T. symptoms can include disorientation for time and place, short attention span, increasingly agitated motor activity, and marked inability to sleep. Tactile hallucinations may also occur, such as feeling snakes crawling up the arms or spiders crawling on the face. There are so many physiological symptoms attached to alcoholism and D.T.'s that a normal physical examination is rare.

Detoxification is an inpatient or hospital procedure, requiring medical management. The patient's condition should be carefully assessed before considering medication. The use of cross-tolerant drugs such as Librium and Valium are often prescribed to assist in easing the withdrawal process. The initial level of Librium or Valium can be decreased 20% each day, until by the fifth day these antianxiety drugs are no longer required. The basis for suggesting such a protocol rests in the fact that convulsions and organic brain syndrome symptoms can be prevented by such procedures, although the incidence of such problems is less than 5% of the general population experiencing withdrawal. Thiamine prescribed for the first two or three days in dosage levels of 100 mg a day is useful to supplement the vitamin deficiencies of most alcoholics. Thiamine has proven to be of some benefit to central and peripheral nervous system development.

Following a relatively brief inpatient treatment program, generally around 30 days, a protracted, prolonged outpatient treatment program and follow-up are almost always indicated (and generally resisted). Emphasis is typically on group therapy, and a very simple approach to group therapy at that. Alcoholics Anonymous seems to provide one of the most useful group intervention programs, emphasizing regular attendance at meetings, regular follow-up and regular personal support. Adjunct medical therapies can include the use of Antabuse, a drug that reacts violently with alcohol. When a patient is taking this drug and decides to imbibe, a very upsetting nauseous reaction occurs. Many alcoholics in treatment are also depressed. Such patients can sometimes profit from focused psychotherapy and antidepressant medication (i.e., tricyclics, heterocyclics, etc.). Note that when a patient is taking antidepressant or tranquilizing medication, his alcohol tolerance will be decreased. That is, it takes less alcohol to get the person intoxicated.

On a final note, be cautious. Never prescribe sleeping medications and steadfastly avoid prescribing antianxiety drugs such as Valium and Librium for your alcoholic patients. Earlier in this chapter we discussed, during the acute detoxification of alcoholic patients; the use of such drugs, but their use was phased out quickly while the patient was still in the hospital. The repeated use of antianxiety drugs simply substitutes one addiction problem for another. You might also bear in mind that alcohol reacts adversely with almost any drug you may prescribe, so be cautious.

The Challenge of Detecting Alcohol Problems: Red Flags

As if you don't already have enough to worry about, be alert to the fact that some research indicates that 30% of all medical/surgical patients are alcoholic. In some settings, such as VA hospitals, this figure can go as high as 80 to 85%! The self-report of patients proved so unreliable in one large metropolitan hospital that the standard elective surgery protocol required a patient to be in the hospital 72 hours before surgery to make certain that an undiagnosed alcoholic didn't have withdrawal symptoms in the recovery room following surgery!

As this example underlines, most patients with an alcohol problem will not identify themselves as problem drinkers. Be sensitive, therefore, to the red flags targeting alcoholism as a potential problem:

1) A spouse may make an appointment for the identified patient for a routine physical exam and the patient will arrive quite sulky, offering no specific complaints whatsoever.

2) When doing your drug and alcohol history, be alert to answers that tend to be too quick, seem blocked or hesitantly given.

3) Be sensitive to such "elastic phrases" as "I drink moderately" or "I can take it or leave it."

4) To avoid putting your patient on the defensive, it is sometimes helpful to ask for a list of prescribed drugs that he has taken recreationally within the last two months. Explain that this information is needed to avoid undesirable drug interactions.

5) During your history, observe if your patient indicates any declining status in his job, the presence of family problems, child abuse, or other social problems.

6) The misuse of alcohol can also be hidden among a wide variety of complaints such as fatigue, nervousness, depression, weight loss and insomnia. The medical history may reveal consistent use of hypnotics and diet pills.

7) In the elderly, confusion and disorientation can well be a product of drug reactions, including alcohol, over-the-counter sleeping aids, hypnotics, and tranquilizers.

When does our job get simple?! Before you get too relaxed, we'll talk about non-alcoholic drugs, but first, let's review.

SUMMARY AND KEY CONCEPTS

Alcoholism is defined as state when alcohol means more to a person than the problems it causes (i.e., significant interference with work, family, and effective functioning). Its **detection and diagnosis** can be assisted by the use of such instruments as the CAGE and MAST checklists.

Alcohol poisons all body systems.

The **clinical course** and natural history of alcoholism is characterized by three factors:

1) Episodic sobriety
2) Spontaneous remission
3) Nonspecific intervention

Treatment of alcoholism from a biomedical and behavioral perspective includes:

1) The medical management of **withdrawal** symptoms
2) Brief **hospitalization** and detoxification
3) Protracted **outpatient** treatment
   (a) Group psychotherapy
   (b) Alcoholics Anonymous
   (c) Antabuse
   (d) Avoidance of cross-tolerant drugs

During your clinical interview and history taking, certain **red flags** may surface indicating possible abuse or dependence on alcohol:

1) Spouse makes appointment for patient who has no specific complaints
2) Elastic phrases about alcohol use
3) Problems with job, family, marriage, etc.
4) Complaints of fatigue, nervousness, and depression
5) Drug reactions

Ready or not, your practice will be impacted by alcohol, a disease we can complain about but can not afford to ignore.

CHAPTER 12

DRUG ABUSE:
THE "HIGHS" THAT BIND

"Let me tell you, people. I know more about the *Physicians' Desk Reference* than most doctors!" he chuckled, as he gave the medical students a knowing look and a condescending smirk. He was a self-proclaimed junkie, a street-wise polydrug abuser who was sharing some of his trade secrets about "croaking" busy doctors. His manufactured symptoms were well designed to mimic illnesses for which he could receive narcotics.

"You guys fall for vague complaints, like a nagging backache from a car accident or a wrenched shoulder from lifting at work. I wait until your waiting room is busy late in the afternoon, claim I don't have any insurance, and offer to pay your receptionist in cash. I'll tell you what drug works best for my "bad back" and stroke you about how busy you are and how I don't want to waste anymore of your time. Hey, I treat you right. After all, you have the keys to the medicine cabinet!"

He was good. Smooth, confident, and convincing. Think about it. There is **no way** that an busy physician up to her ears in patients could match the energy and take the time to ferret out such a con man. And such a patient represents only one kind of drug abuser.

Types of Drug Abusers

Dr. Al Carlin, a clinical psychologist at the University of Washington School of Medicine who has worked for decades with drug abuse, identifies four groups of abusers and the drugs involved:

1) **Streetwise illicit drug users** use cocaine, methaqualone, methadone, opiates and synthetic narcotics.

2) **Street persons** with low financial and social resources abuse inhalants, codeine, amphetamines, and hallucinogenics.
3) **Recreational abusers** use marijuana, amphetamines, and hallucinogenics.
4) **Straight persons** attempting to self-medicate for depression or anxiety tend to use barbiturates and minor tranquilizers.

The diagnosis of drug abuse must rely on more than superficial factors of appearance and grooming, and treatment must take into account not only the substance involved but also the function served by the pattern of use.

Definitions of Drug Abuse

Drug abuse may be defined in several ways. The **social** definition includes any pattern of drug use that is frowned upon by society. This involves both the substance used and how it is used. The **legal** definition of drug abuse includes any pattern of use violating statutory law. Often these laws are the result of previous societal concerns. Perhaps more useful to physicians is a **medical** definition of drug abuse i.e., any pattern of drug use that jeopardizes the user's health or psychological, social, or fiscal functioning. Thus, the medical definition is based on deleterious consequences rather than the substance involved, chronicity, frequency, or social reputation.

An abusable drug is one that **changes thinking or mood** quickly enough to be recognized by the user. Intoxication by any drug depends not only on the **physiologic effects,** but also on the **user's expectations** and the **setting** in which the drug is used.

Drug Classes, Behavioral Profiles, and Treatments

For your studying convenience, the following information about representative drug classes, their behavioral symptoms, and possible treatments will be presented in an outline format. Don't freak out about memorizing this information. Just bask in the awareness of the vast array of chemicals out there that can screw up your patients, test your diagnostic acumen, and challenge your treatment repertoire.

1) **Stimulants** (i.e., amphetamines/methamphetamines)
Behavioral presentation: Hyperactive, can experience intense euphoria and delusions of grandeur; may have paranoid characteristics; typically deny drugs are the cause of their feeling state. After "coming down" (2-3 days), there is often a refractory depression (7-21 days).
Treatment: Permit patient to "sleep it off;" may require tranquilizers such as benzodiazepines to "come down." Overdose can be fatal; withdrawal is not.

2) **Sedative-hypnotics** (i.e., barbiturates, benzodiazepines)
   Behavioral presentation: Looks drunk, no odor of alcohol, slurred speech, ataxia, impaired social judgment, etc.
   Emergency room treatment: Clear the airway, support vital signs, begin titrated withdrawal; Sometimes lavage followed by an activated charcoal bolus.
   Treatment: Persons addicted to sedative hypnotics can die from withdrawal or overdose. Must be withdrawn by titrated doses under medical supervision. Withdrawal may result in a toxic delirium and seizures.
3) **Narcotics** (i.e., heroin)
   Behavioral presentation: Within the first 15 minutes after injection, toxic patients manifest sleepy behavior (e.g., nodding, "kissing the table", etc.) They can be aroused by calling their name or shaking them.
   Narcotic Abstinence Syndrome: pilo-erection, rhinorrhea, pupillary dilation, diarrhea. Sometimes "trackmarks" of needles.
   Related diseases: Hepatitis, abscesses, pulmonary complications, overdose, hemorrhoids, GI tract disturbance, bacteria endocarditis, HIV infection.
   Treatment of overdose: Clear airway, support vital signs, administration of antagonists (e.g., Naloxone [narcan]. Patients rarely die from withdrawal but can die from overdose.
4) **Marijuana**
   Behavioral presentation: Euphoria, increased appetite, decreased intraocular pressure, nausea suppression, doesn't dilate pupils. Sometimes symptoms of tachycardia, bronchial dilation, REM sleep suppression, suppression of cell mediated immune response, pain suppression, nausea suppression, and infection of the conjunctiva.
   a) Significant impairment of memory
   b) Because it is lipophilic, effects can be demonstrated weeks after use is ended.
   c) Amotivational syndrome: Major motivation is to get the drug, and all else is secondary. Seems to have no energy or drive.
   Treatment: Need for medical intervention is rare; referral to outpatient drug treatment program if chronic user.
5) **Psychedelics** (LSD, mescaline, peyote, STP)
   Behavioral Presentation: Disorganized thinking, fearful, auditory and visual hallucinations, signs of schizophrenia.
   Treatment: Neuroleptics not recommended because of possible synergistic effects on the cardiovascular and respiratory systems.
6) **Phencyclidine** (PCP)
   Behavioral presentation: Catatonia, combative, convulsions, and coma; vertical and/or lateral nystagmus.

In summarizing the above findings, the consequences of dysfunctional drug use may include:

1) **Panic reactions:** Dysphoria, anxiety attacks
2) **Toxic effects:** Acute brain syndrome, psychosis, sedation, coma, respiratory depression, etc.
3) **Tolerance:** Increased dosage required for the same effect
4) **Physical dependence:** Stopping use results in withdrawal symptoms
5) **Psychological dependence:** Effects of positive and negative reinforcement
6) **Psychosis:** Often a function of the patient's and culture's previous experience with the substance
7) **Physical sequilae:** Often due to accidents because of an altered mental state

Personality Characteristics of Drug Abusers

Drugs are used and misused by a wide variety of people and for a wide variety of reasons. An addictive personality as such has not been demonstrated to exist. Although some drug abusers might be classified as personality disorders, the vast majority do not conveniently fit any behavioral, medical, or psychological category. Personality characteristics frequently associated with chemical abusers include:

1) **Low self-esteem** (e.g., don't feel as good as, etc.)
2) **External locus of control:** The person depends on external events to control his life (e.g., the bottle is empty or the bar closes).
3) **Avoidance** of unpleasant or negative feeling states (e.g., "When life's a "downer", I'm on an upper!")

A Caution to Physicians

Apart from being conned by the streetwise drug user, you yourself must take care to avoid inadvertently addicting your patients to psychoactive drugs. Physicians can limit these iatrogenic (Rush to the dictionary!) risks by avoiding drugs with a highly addictive potential (e.g., fast-acting drugs with rapid onset of tranquilizing or stimulating effects) and by not prescribing usage on a PRN or "as needed" basis. Prescribing long-acting medications on a fixed time schedule (e.g., "Take once at 9:00 a.m. and once at 3:00 p.m. and once at bedtime") can neutralize the vicious conditioning cycle set up by psychoactive drugs taken on a PRN ("as needed") basis (Review our discussion of medication in the section on Chronic Pain, pages 54-55). You should be aware that some patients are especially susceptible to medication: those with previous addiction history; those who are antisocial, impulsive, and irresponsible; and those who have little insight into their own behavior or could "care less."

Whenever a patient requests or requires the prescription of a potentially addictive medication, try to determine if your patient is a high addiction risk. Get the names of other physicians and pharmacists who have treated this patient and contact them. Pain complaints should be assessed to see if they are acute and medically plausible. Many sophisticated drug abusers, as indicated earlier, have a "working knowledge" of the PDR, feigning target symptoms to get their drug of choice. Be cautious of practical issues, such as having your narcotics license printed on your prescription pad. Such a pad, complete with this "combination to the medicine cabinet," is easy to steal. The problem of license number security is readily resolved: Add your number in longhand.

In general, the treatment of chemical dependence begins with inpatient crisis intervention, the inpatient therapeutic community which often uses the Twelve Step philosophy, and medication. As treatment progresses to an outpatient setting, crisis intervention may still be indicated with "slips." A supportive therapeutic community remains central to therapeutic improvement, but the role of medication support is phased out.

Actual treatment of bona fide drug abusers requires highly trained and experienced professionals made from a special cloth. This world of drug abuse is not a logical world built on reason and planning. Frequently it's an emotional jungle with intrapsychic predators that would make Steven Spielberg shudder. It's a world that requires unbelievable energy to engage, papal patience, and a commitment to "wait until the Fat Lady sings." Our best advice: Treat the acute physical needs of the abuser, and then refer to drug treatment programs with staff who "know the territory" of the toxic brains, tortured psyches, and riddled relationships of the chemically dependent.

SUMMARY AND KEY CONCEPTS

Carlin provides a helpful description of four **types of drug abusers** and their drugs of choice (Check pages 77-78 for a description of the latter):

1) Streetwise illicit drug users
2) Street persons
3) Recreational abusers
4) Straight persons

A working definition of an **abusable drug** is one that changes thinking or mood quickly enough to be recognized by the user. Intoxication by any drug depends not only on the physiologic effects, but also on the user's expectations and the setting in which the drug is used.

Behavioral profiles of representative **drug classes** and their respective treatments include the following:

1) Stimulants
2) Sedative-hypnotics
3) Narcotics
4) Marijuana

5) Psychedelics
6) Phencyclidine

The **consequences of dysfunctional drug usage** are sobering, and can involve:

1) Panic reactions
2) Toxic reactions
3) Tolerance
4) Physical and psychological dependence
5) Psychosis
6) Accidents

Strategies to avoid iatrogenic addiction (What in the world is "iatrogenic addiction?" "Physician-caused" perhaps?):

1) Avoid prescription drugs with fast acting onset of tranquilizing or stimulating effects.
2) Prescribe for a fixed time schedule rather than taking "as needed", i.e., PRN.
3) If suspicious of drug misuse, check with your patient's other physicians and pharmacists.
4) If suspicious of drug misuse, re-evaluate the objective basis of the patient's symptoms and complaints, and review the need for potentially addicting medication.
5) Develop a working relationship with local and regional drug treatment programs.
6) Unless you are committed to learning the complex psychological and physiological territory traveled by the drug abuser, refer to a professional who is! There is no shame in working with others!

CHAPTER 13

DISORDERS OF SLEEP: CORTICAL COBWEBS AND CALAMITY

If there was a problem that was involved each year in killing between ten and twenty thousand Americans, caused one third of our nation's fatal truck accidents, was implicated in many disasters (a space shuttle explosion, the *Exxon Valdez* oil spill, and the nuclear catastrophes at Chernobyl and Three Mile Island), wouldn't everyone consider it a profound health hazard? Such a disorder is not imaginary. It exists and is invisible, and it is undiagnosed, misdiagnosed, or mistreated 99% of the time. So concludes Dr. William Dement, an international authority on sleep and the Director of the Stanford University Sleep Center. He estimates that there are 40 million undiagnosed and untreated chronically ill sleep disorder patients, some of whom account for the above mentioned tragedies.

America is a 24-hour-a-day society . . . we don't value or respect sleep. As a result, the primary cause of many disastrous accidents goes unheeded. A third mate was fatigued and sleep deprived, fell "asleep on his feet," and the *Exxon Valdez* ran aground, causing one of the worst environmental disasters in history. Prior to the fatal launch of the space shuttle *Challenger,* senior NASA managers had been awake for 36 hours without sleep. The Rogers Commission concluded that the launch was an erroneous decision that cost the lives of the Challenger crew and $50 billion. According to the National Transportation Safety Board, the leading cause of fatal truck accidents is fatigue/sleep deprivation (31%). General highway fatalities due to sleep deprivation are conservatively estimated to be between 10,000 to 20,000 people each year. Yet few driver's education courses ever talk about driving when drowsy. Tragically, teenagers need on the average of 9.2 hours of sleep a night or they are in sleep deprivation. Have you ever known a teenager who sleeps 9.2 hours a night? No way! Yet the effects of sleep deprivation can overtake us all as rapidly and as irresistibly as a seizure. Shift workers are notoriously sleep deprived, and such deprivation led to the night-shift nuclear catastrophes of Chernobyl and Three Mile Island.

And the practice of medicine? According to a recent University of California survey, 41% of physicians on staff at major hospitals were "too tired to concentrate," a problem directly linked to patients' deaths. Yet interns and residents routinely are expected to stand 36 hour shifts and 120 hour weeks. We are a sleep deprived society.

Yet falling asleep is not an act of God. This action is considered negligence by the Court. Trial lawyers are now becoming sleep specialists: If it can be established that sleepiness or falling asleep caused damages, there is liability. Sleep is a drive, like hunger and thirst. The sleep drive can be suppressed but not eliminated. Alertness and drowsiness are central issues in human behavior. Drowsiness is the last step before sleep.

Definitions of Sleep

What is sleep? It is an active disengagement from our environment. Our brain shuts out sensory input; we cease to be aware of the outer world and turn toward the inner world. At the moment of sleep, we become instantaneously blind and deaf. Our external perceptual processes disengage, our brain waves change, eye movement slows, we experience hypnogogic imagery, and the gate between short-term and long-term memory closes. Electrographically, sleep is characterized by a shift from the normal waking state of high frequency, low amplitude brain waves to various states of low frequency, high amplitude brain waves. In particular, normal sleep consists of several cyclings through REM (rapid eye movement) sleep and four stages of NREM sleep (Stages 1 through 4).

REM and NREM Sleep

REM Sleep occurs about four or five times in a night's sleep and is characterized by:

1) Functional paralysis
   a) Torso muscles in state of total relaxation except for some finger, toe, limb twitches.
   b) Facial grimaces
2) Rapid, darting eye movements
3) Erratic breathing and heart rate
4) Erections in men and vasocongestion in women
5) The lateral geniculate of the thalamus receives volleys of information from the pons. From the thalamus the information travels to the cortex. Another path goes from the pons to the medulla and spinal cord.
6) Nerve tissue shows peak growth patterns with such stimulation.

When awakened from REM sleep, most persons report vivid, detailed **dreams.** An adequate amount of REM sleep appears to be important to healthy functioning; persons deprived of REM sleep develop a "REM debt" which they make up in ensuing sleep sessions. Many common drugs, including alcohol, disrupt REM sleep and may thereby contribute to sleep disturbance.

Stages 1 and 2 of **NREM Sleep** consist of a light sleep, whereas stages 3 and 4 are known as deep or slow-wave sleep. Stages 3 and 4 occur two or three times in an evening's sleep, but are rare in the early morning hours.

Stage 1: Low voltage of mixed frequency but most predominant is Theta (4-8 cycles per second). Similar to experienced meditators.

Stage 2: Spindles of 12-14 cps, with random spikes.

Stage 3 and 4: Slow wave, mainly Delta (<4 cps; high amplitude; very deep sleep).

How quickly we fall asleep (sleep latency) is an objective measure of physiological sleepiness or sleep deprivation. People in the "twilight zone" may not feel sleepy, but, as the sleep deprivation accidents indicate, being awake is not the same as being alert. Always pay attention to drowsiness! A large sleep debt creates daily zones of vulnerability from apathy, inattention, microsleep, and unintended sleep episodes, resulting in errors, accidents, death, and catastrophes. Driving when drowsy is not significantly different from driving when drunk!

Sleep Disorders

Let's consider several sleep disorders which will be common to your medical practice:

Insomnia (Disorders of Initiating or Maintaining Sleep, or DIMS) is one of the most common complaints in general medical practice, afflicting perhaps 30% of the normal population. Several factors may contribute to insomnia:

Situational stressors (e.g., job problems, marital discord)
Aging (Older persons generally sleep less well)
Drugs (Especially caffeine and alcohol, and withdrawal from some drugs)
Psychiatric disorders (Especially schizophrenia and affective disorders)

Treatment for insomnia can be summarized along four dimensions: Psychotherapy, medication, behavioral intervention, and sleep hygiene strategies:

1) **Psychotherapy** can involve learning the cognitive control of negative thoughts, and learning to express affect during the waking hours. It may also involve dream therapy.

2) **Medication** treatment needs to be approached with caution, given some of the time-limited efficacy of certain drugs, drugs which can rapidly become part of the problem instead of part of the solution. If you choose to prescribe, consider the following drug effects:
   a) Tricyclic antidepressants: reduce REM sleep
   b) Benzodiazepines: reduce time in Delta sleep
   c) Caffeine and diet pills: delay sleep onset
   d) Alcohol: initial depressant effect followed in 4 hours by alerting effect
   e) Sleep meds: increase sleep length but not sleep quality; tolerance develops within 3 weeks to 3 months

3) **Behavioral intervention strategies:**
   a) Progressive relaxation techniques
   b) Biofeedback: EMG (muscle) feedback, particularly in the initial stages of relaxation training, may prove particularly helpful in developing a relaxation response which is a precursor to sleep.
   c) Sleep restriction: Patient allowed to be in bed only for the average amount of time he has been recorded to have slept in previous nights.
   d) Stimulus control: If not asleep within 20 minutes, get out of bed for 20 minutes and repeat until patient falls asleep quickly.
   e) Hot bath several hours before bed

4) **Sleep hygiene techniques:**
   a) Regular sleep-wake schedule
   b) Reduced light and noise
   c) Eliminate caffeine, smoking, alcohol
   d) Cool room
   e) Exercise during the day
   f) Reduce activity at night

Hypersomnia (Disorders of Excessive Somnolence) encompasses a variety of sleep disorders whose common characteristic is **excessive sleepiness.** Hypersomnia may be the presenting complaint in narcolepsy, Kleine-Levin syndrome, and sleep apnea.

Narcolepsy typically occurs before age 40 and includes one or more of the following symptoms:

1) Sleep attacks
2) Hallucinations
3) Cataplexy
4) Sleep paralysis

All narcoleptic patients suffer from **sleep attacks,** which can be a very disabling symptom. A patient may fall asleep while dancing, piloting an airplane, performing surgery, eating a meal, driving, talking to friends, or engaging in sexual intercourse. (This last symptom runs the risk of being forcibly kicked out of bed in an unceremonious fashion by an irate partner.) Sleep attacks vary in their phenomenology and duration but commonly last about fifteen minutes. Visual or auditory **hallucinations** may precede sleep or occur during the sleep attack. **Cataplexy** consists of a sudden loss of muscle tone, which can range from localized muscle weakness to a total physical collapse and paralysis. Cataplexy is often initiated by an emotional outburst such as laughing, crying, or anger. This state may last anywhere from a few seconds to 30 minutes. **Sleep paralysis** consists of flaccid muscle tone with full consciousness; this state occurs during awakening or while falling asleep. The paralysis does not last long and dissipates gradually or when the patient is touched.

In the **Kleine-Levin syndrome,** hypersomnic attacks may last up to 20 hours but occur infrequently, perhaps three to four times a year. Upon awakening, the patient is confused. This syndrome is separate and distinct from narcolepsy, in which the hypersomnia is much more frequent and of much shorter duration.

In **sleep apnea,** the two key symptoms are

1) Loud snoring at night and
2) Excessive sleepiness during the day. In addition, persons with this affliction show decreased attention span, decreased memory, and hyperirritability.

In **central apnea,** there is a cessation of respiratory movement with loss of airflow. In **obstructive apnea,** there is a persistent respiratory effort but upper airway blockage. Apneic episodes may occur dozens or hundreds of times in an evening, so sleep is badly fragmented.
   Treatment for sleep apnea may involve:

1) Behavioral intervention: Helpful techniques include sleep position training, weight loss, exercise and alcohol reduction.
2) Mechanical intervention: In an effort to clear the patient's airway during sleep, such instruments as tongue retaining devices and nasal continuous positive airway pressure (NCPAP) procedures may be used.
3) Surgery: Depending on the anatomical status of the patient, some forms of sleep apnea can be surgically treated with a tonsillectomy, submucous resection to open the nasal airway, uvulopalatal pharyngeoplasty, mandibular advancement and tracheostomy.

Additional sleep disorders that are more common in children include **enuresis** (bed-wetting), **somnambulism** (sleepwalking), and **pavor nocturnus** (night terrors). In a night terror, the child awakens abruptly, screaming with fright, and may stand up in bed or run around the room. The child is also disoriented, appears to experience hallucinations of animals or strange people, and does not recognize his or her parents. Night terrors are most common in young children, who may be amnesic for the event. Although they are very distressing to parents, night terrors do not necessarily signify emotional problems, and children generally outgrow them.

Although not as impressive as more exotic diseases, sleep disorders can have a profound effect on your patients' lives. In fact, keep an eye on your own sleep debt. No need to add to the tragic accidents already documented and attributed to this invisible threat to so many.

SUMMARY AND KEY CONCEPTS

The failure to adequately diagnose and treat sleep disorders has resulted in significant tragedy. This chapter reviews definitions of sleep, and the characteristics of REM and NREM sleep. In addition, we discuss sleep disorders, including:

1) Insomnia
2) Hypersomnia
3) Narcolepsy
4) Kleine-Levin syndrome
5) Sleep Apnea
6) Sleep disorders common to children: (a) Enuresis, (b) Somnambulism, (c) Pavor nocturnus and (d) Sandman on vacation (Just kidding!)

CHAPTER 14

THE TRAGEDIES OF DOMESTIC VIOLENCE: BROKEN HEARTS

"Me Tarzan, You jane!" No typographical mistake here. In many cultures, the spelling is Jane with a small *j*. Whatever the capitalization, the message remains the same: The female part of this couple is "lower case"—Testosterone rules! And when the power dynamics of this structure are challenged, particularly by the "weaker sex," body bruises and broken hearts may result. Although domestic abuse can occur with men as the victims, the vast majority of abused partners are women (i.e., 94%). The physical power differential is compelling: The war of the sexes is an unequal one, with men wielding battle-axes and women swinging sticks.

In spite of civilized attempts to emphasize the humane in humanity, domestic violence has been accepted, sanctioned, and even legalized within most cultures since the dawn of time—regardless of its devastating impact on families and individuals. From the Bible to British Common Law, women have traditionally been treated as children. In nineteenth-century Great Britain, for example, spousal discipline was governed by "The Rule of Thumb," i.e., the "switch" used on a wife couldn't be any larger in diameter than the husband's thumb. This rule was actually considered a reform, according to English philosopher John Stuart Mill. Men were expected to be strong, reactive, and physically forceful. The women's suffrage movement in the 1800's struck a spark that slowly ignited feminist action against spousal discipline. The Women's Movement in the 1960's, the sexual revolution, the Civil Rights Movement . . . all heightened social concern for women's issues. History records a long and enduring chronicle of women's struggles with domestic violence and its often untold effects on the lives and deaths of women.

You've heard in the national media the chilling statistics of domestic violence:

In 15 million families, violence has taken place at least once.

2,000 to 4,000 women die each year because of domestic violence.

40% female and 10% male homicides are killings committed by their partners.

Each 15 seconds a woman is beaten.

Every day four battered women die.

Here's another sobering fact that may strike closer to home: The probability of your dealing in your practice with a victim of violence is 100%, although you may not know it until after the fact. Of every 27 women admitted to the emergency room for abuse, only one is diagnosed as having abuse-related injuries.

These statistics are shocking. More startling, however, is the fact that many women do not report cases of abuse for a variety of reasons, some of which include guilt and shame, societal acceptance of abuse, being perceived as a loser, and being viewed as a participant unless evidence exists to the contrary (i.e., guilty of participation unless proven otherwise).

Myths and Facts about Domestic Violence

In our culture, a raft of unsubstantiated opinion and folklore flourish about fighting within the family. Myths abound about domestic violence:

Myth: "She must like it or she wouldn't put up with it."

Fact: Nobody likes to be beaten, bruised and broken. Nobody.

Forget Hollywood and what the movies portray. Abused partners frequently are **frightened** partners. They are frightened not only of physical or emotional abuse but of being alone, unable to support themselves (and their children). Generally, they have minimal job skills, no self-confidence and no reliable support system. Typical characteristics of a victim of abuse include:

1) Low self-esteem

2) Depression

3) Dependency on the marital role for one's personal identity (i.e., "I'm just a wife.")

4) Rigid sex role definition: "Me Tarzan, you etc."

5) Feeling backed into a corner with no options but the abusive relationship

6) May neglect children within the abusive primary relationship

7) Victim taking primary responsibility for the abuse and the fate of the relationship

Myth: Battery is a nonwhite, low socioeconomic status problem.

Fact: Domestic violence occurs at every level of our society.

It is not limited to the poor, but is seen in all classes including lower, middle, and upper economic levels. Research indicates that it is poor women who are more likely to leave an abusive relationship than women of any other socioeconomic level.

Myth: She incited his violence.
Fact: The "She-devil" didn't make him do it. He did it.

Unfortunately, intimate interpersonal relationships in the U.S. are bathed in some rather poisonous expectations regarding violence. Violence is viewed as a solution to interpersonal problems. In fact, violence is seemingly regarded as a requirement of the socialization process (e.g., The majority of Americans polled in several recent studies approve striking children as a viable form of discipline). And then there is the electronic, mindless Cyclops that spends more time with our kids than do we or their classroom teachers. The average American child will have observed 20,000 murders on television before he or she is 18 years of age. How's that for role modeling future relationships?! Tarzan and Jane are rather tame compared with the *Fatal Attraction* couples displayed on the Tube. For many, the family no longer functions to insure survival. It no longer provides the nurturing necessary for emotional, physical and intellectual growth. The family is not available to many as an effective stress buffer. In the 1990's our culture's "family portrait" no longer provides appropriate social role models. *Ozzie and Harriet* or *Leave it to Beaver* may have been sketched in saccharin, but at least they were not choking or shooting their lovers in the bedroom while the kids looked on.

Patterns of Domestic Violence

The "landscape" for abusive patterns generally involves several features:

1) Abuse most likely involves a male battering a female, although some victim precipitation may appear present.
2) The sites for battering are usually in the home, with the kitchen and bedroom equally preferred.
3) Early to late evening are prime times for battering.
4) Fridays and weekends are the high risk days for violence.
5) Older adults typically are not present, as their presence seems to lessen the value of anger as an excuse for violence.

The consequences of domestic violence are chilling:

81% of the victims are visibly injured.
Domestic violence accounts for 30% of law enforcement fatalities.
40% of all murders stem from family violence.

Less lethal domestic violence behaviors may take the form of emotional neglect, verbal abuse, physical restraint, surrogate abuse (e.g., kicking the dog) and well as the more extreme physical battering.

The Battering Cycle

Battering within an abusive relationship does not usually occur on a continuous daily basis. The **battering cycle** itself, as described by domestic relations expert Lenore Walker, occurs in three phases:

1) **tension buildup**
2) the **explosion** or **acute battering**
3) the resolution, contrition, and **loving respite** phase.

The length or frequency of each phase cannot be reliably predicted. Varied levels of psychological abuse occur during the first phase, and physical violence occurs in the explosion phase, accompanied by severe levels of physical and psychological abuse. This is commonly followed by the batterer's extreme desire to appear remorseful for his actions, as he behaves in a loving and caring manner towards his partner. The abused spouse truly has the desire to believe the abuse will not occur again. The wife is socialized to keep the family unit intact, to be a good mother, and to accept responsibility when something goes wrong in the marriage. Elements of this third phase reinforce everything that happens before and provides the "glue" that keeps the relationship together. Tragically, abusive episodes then occur more frequently and become more severe. Far from being "stupid," the victim learns to intervene earlier, using interventions that delay the escalation of violence because she "pushes his buttons" earlier in the process. She becomes like the semi-truck driver who averts a head-on collision by hitting the ditch. The victim tries to sidestep a head-on assault by precipitating a crisis that may result in fewer injuries. What a choice! Some victims can become quite skillful in driving this highway, learning painful survival strategies that only partially and temporarily work, but seemingly dodge disaster for the moment.

Treatment and Management

What to do about these impending domestic collisions? Your role in the medical management of domestic violence encompasses more than the diagnosis and treatment of the injuries encountered in the battering incident. It is often difficult to "interfere" in such incidents for they are of a family nature and could possibly lead to threats or injury to you or your staff. It is important to examine your personal feelings, values, and beliefs in order to render the best possible care, for these crises are as critical as any life-threatening situation in your practice. A **thorough assessment** and description of such injuries is necessary, not only for solid medical care but because your medical records may be required as legal evidence. One example of the value of such thoroughness in assessment involved a study that examined an emergency trauma service and found that one in twenty women initially reported an occurrence of domestic violence related to their injuries. In actuality, when the data were reexamined, it was found that one in four women experienced what would be considered domestic abuse.

During your evaluation and diagnosis of the patient, do not be surprised or be put off by patient guardedness, or by her return to the batterer or her repeated victimization. You need to **understand** what it is like to walk in her shoes. Therefore, it generally is helpful to interview the patient alone without any accompanying person. Time is needed to permit a thorough interview, diagnosis, and assessment. When possible, hospitalization is recommended for recovery from serious physical and psychological injuries, as well as for respite and refuge. Hospitalization allows both the identified victim and the batterer to deal with the consequences of abuse. If hospitalization does not occur it is important for the professional to express the seriousness of the injuries and the abuse pattern. It is also important for professionals to be aware of safe homes, refuges and shelters within the area that can provide an immediate safe haven for the victim. Physical relocation can minimize the victim being returned in a vulnerable state to the scene of the crime. Often, battered women will follow the advice of professionals if such advice appears sound, sensible, and workable. Relying on familial and friendship support systems may not always be an appropriate means of assistance, because the batterer may threaten them if the wife does not return home. Therefore, you may be required to have more knowledge of **community support systems** i.e.,

1) Escort services to safe homes, refuges, and shelters
2) The procedures and protocols used by social service agencies (i.e., intake, care for children, length of stay, cost etc.). This information can assist in alleviating additional fears the victims may be experiencing for seeking professional services.
3) Counseling agencies
4) Legal services within the community as well as other support agencies

These services allow women to make independent decisions regarding their welfare and future.

The **medical management** of battering victims is a challenge that will touch you deeply, both professionally and personally. Several basic treatment steps should be kept in mind:

1) Expect your victimized patient to be **guarded in her fear,** intimidated in her **conflicted** intimate relationship, and torn between sharing with you her emotional dilemma or returning to her abusing partner.
2) Focus on initially viewing your patient's conflicts through her eyes as you practice **empathy.** Your compassionate understanding can move her a long way in staring down her deeply felt fears and misgivings. It is remarkably healing for a victim to know that someone she respects can actually comprehend what it is like to be caught in the domestic abuse cycle. Domestic abuse is not a logical problem. It is an emotional dilemma of unprecedented complexity, a

dilemma that pulls a victim apart emotionally: The vary hands that hold her close in a warm embrace are the same hands that bloody and bruise her body. . . and her heart. With your compassionate, empathetic response to her emotionally entangled predicament, she can gain an emotional "toe hold." She can begin to challenge her misperceptions about her abusive relationship, perceive her intimate reality more clearly, and start taking steps to extricate herself from the tar pit or trap of abuse.

3) Do not hesitate to make immediate appropriate **referrals** to sheltered care and to mental health professionals familiar with battering. Seek consultation yourself if you feel uncomfortable in dealing with the complicated morass called domestic violence.

4) **Follow up** with your patient when it is possible and appropriate. Abuse victims need regular contact with supportive professionals and friends who truly care about their well-being.

Through such efforts, women learn to break the cycle of violence, to live without fear, and to lead positive and productive lives. Future generations will learn that intimate relationships need not be governed by laws of the reptilian brain. Individuals as well as families can learn to live without the detrimental consequences of domestic violence. The cry of Tarzan and the violence of the jungle need not be our metaphors for intimate relationships. Yet domestic violence continues as a modern social problem that presently cries out in a civilized society for recognition and the need for a solution. Doctor, help find it.

SUMMARY AND KEY CONCEPTS

Domestic violence has **historical roots** that run deep, with emotional traps that prove more compelling than logical solutions. Be aware of the **myths** that surrounding domestic violence, as well as the **landscape** within which such violence occurs.

The **battering cycle** involves three components:

1) Tension buildup
2) Explosion or acute battering
3) Loving respite phase

After treatment of the victim's physical injuries, proper **medical management** of domestic violence includes:

1) Understanding of a frightened, emotionally conflicted patient.
2) Empathy for the victim. Be cautious about premature advice.
3) Working knowledge of viable referral resources.
4) Appropriate follow-up.

CHAPTER 15

SEXUAL ABUSE: THE INTIMATE WOUND

Her eight-year-old eyes were filled with tears.

"What seems to be the trouble?" the doctor asked, observing that the girl winced with pain when sitting down on the chair.

"Nothing," she replied. Her chart indicated that she had been missing school and had tried to run away from home twice within the last several months. Her affect was mildly dysphoric and withdrawn. Physical examination revealed no bruises on her body, except for tenderness and pain in her pelvic area.

This case reveals some **short-term behavioral symptoms** in children of sexual abuse, symptoms which may include:

> Mood disturbance: depression, anxiety, irritability, phobias
> Sleep disorder
> Pain in genital area
> Difficulty walking or sitting
> Inappropriate sexual behaviors
> Truancy
> Running away

Additional **physical symptoms** may involve (1) genital or anal trauma, (2) sexually transmitted disease, and (3) urinary tract infection.

Sexual abuse is a term that describes a wide range of sexually exploitive activities, none of which you look forward to seeing in your practice. As is the case in so much of what you will treat as a physician, you are the first line of intervention, like it or not. The victims of sexual abuse, and sometimes the perpetrators, will seek you out and will need your help.

95

There are several legal and clinical issues regarding age, consent, victim and perpetrator. For health care professionals, the problems associated with sexual abuse have many biopsychosocial implications with extensive short-term and long-term health consequences. Typically, **sexual abuse** is defined as any sexual act towards an unwilling victim (i.e., forcible rape) and/or victim who is mentally and legally unable to give consent (statutory rape). Generally, sexually exploitive acts are identified as (1) incest, (2) molestation, (3) assault, or (4) rape. This definition does not usually address or identify sexual deviations which can include masochism, sadism, bestiality, and necrophilia.

Sexual abuse towards others may or may not include violence. In fact, data indicate that only **5 to 10%** of sexually abused victims actually show **signs of physical injury** when examined medically. Nevertheless, since victims are most commonly **female,** family practice physicians and pediatricians are advised to maintain regular documentation of the hymenal area when performing routine physical examinations with prepubertal females and pay particular attention to hymenal sizes that deviate substantially from previously obtained baselines. Recent studies show nonabused hymen size remains constant with stable variance over development and is not substantially influenced by height, weight, or age for those under 12. Although results also indicate a slightly larger hymenal area for those who masturbate, the same homogeneous stable standard deviation exists for those with no history of sexual abuse. Research shows that females are **10 times** more likely to become victims than males. The most **commonly molested child** is a female between the ages of 7 through 12.

Perpetrators are usually males in their thirties who abuse alcohol and/or drugs, although they are not necessarily limited to this profile. Typically a family member or friend, only **10%** of the perpetrators are strangers. When perpetrators are fathers or father substitutes, psychological effects tend to be more traumatic and extensive.

Earlier we outlined some of the short-term symptoms of molestation. **Long-term behavioral consequences** may include:

>Delinquency
>Drug abuse
>Poor heterosexual relations
>Prostitution
>Sexual promiscuity
>Guilt
>Shame
>Depression
>Social withdrawal
>Years of emotional scars lasting into adulthood

Several **adjustment patterns** typical of the sexually abused have been identified:

1) **Avoidance:** Victim refuses to discuss events; remains fearful of adults; experiences self-blame, guilt, and self-doubt leading to frequent psychological distress.

2) **Repetition:** Victim revisits her victimization by sexually acting out, continuing her self-blame, experiencing frequent anxiety, and exhibiting poor relationships with her peers and family.

3) **Identification:** Victim copes with sexual trauma by identifying with her perpetrator, becoming antisocial and angry towards others, displaying sexually deviant behavior, maintaining relations with the exploiter, and blaming authorities.

4) **Integration:** Victim effectively copes with anxiety, blames her perpetrator and believes that he should be punished.

Unfortunately, the psychological scarring from these illegal acts may manifest themselves in physical symptoms. One case study reveals that a 35-year-old woman who had been repeatedly molested for thirty years by her stepfather complained to several physicians of numbness in her extremities. Several surgeries produced no relief. After years of psychotherapy, she finally revealed incest to her therapist. Her stepfather would hold her arms down tightly while molesting her, and she described feelings of detachment in her arms whenever he would touch her.

Appreciate that sometimes physical symptoms are signals from the patient's body of underlying emotional/psychological distress. These **conversion reactions** are not as farfetched as they initially may seem. Physical symptoms are generally more socially acceptable, whereas psychological and emotional problems seem to retain a more negative stigma.

Another case of sexual molestation involved a patient complaining of shortness of breath, labored breathing, and hyperventilation. Medical tests showed her heart rate was normal, and there appeared no reasons for the breathing difficulty. Psychotheraphy later revealed father-daughter incest, and holding her breath was a guarding response to her fear of her father's unknown and undesired advances. She used this conditioned breathing pattern to cope in her father's presence.

Psychiatric disorders can also become symptomatic of sexual abuse, as seen with a patient who presented "trichotillomania." This condition involves the learned self-abuse of removing hair from the scalp or eyebrows in a nervous hair-pulling habit. This obsessive and compulsive ritual is literally pulling out one's hair. In this case, the patient served as the family placater and sought to maintain family harmony at her own expense. She was sexually abused by her father for several years. Ironically, she felt responsible for seeking help for the family and requested family psychotherapy.

Medical professionals need not be reminded that crimes against children represent one of the most repulsive areas of medicine. The range of abuse may include death of a child, as with the "battered child syndrome," or a normal maturing adolescent who may want your support in helping explain to her father not to hold, touch, or play physically as they once did when she was young. Children may benefit from protection and from instruction on their rights regarding their bodies. Yet, we must also not be afraid to touch. We need not sacrifice or discourage one of our most basic human needs. Simply teaching "good" touching and "bad" touching may only teach children that the issue is too complicated, leading them to choose not to touch at all. Each family has its own patterns and rules of conduct with appropriate behaviors in these sensitive areas. It is important that professionals recognize the signs, symptoms, and pleas for help, no matter how weak or obvious they may seem.

Children who report sexual abuse are often not believed and are made to feel guilty. On the other hand, our country is also in the midst of a great hysteria concerning child protection. Some cases are indeed fabricated, and manipulative methods are used to remove children from spousal custody during divorce or separation. Careful, thorough, and sensitive investigations, sound medical evidence, accurate physician testimony, and trained health protection professionals are essential in combating this serious social and health problem. Legally and ethically, **all child sexual abuse must be reported to child welfare authorities.** All reported or suspected cases of sexual abuse are to be taken seriously with mindful appreciation of the many social, physical, psychological, and family complexities.

SUMMARY AND KEY CONCEPTS

Although the sexual abuse of children is an odious clinical reality, your sensitivity to such pathology can be enhanced by your awareness of the following.

Short-term behavior signs and physical symptoms:

1) Mood disturbances
    a) Depression
    b) Anxiety
    c) Irritability
    d) Phobias
2) Sleep disorder
3) Pain in genital area
4) Difficulty walking or sitting
5) Inappropriate sexual behavior
6) Truancy
7) Running away
8) Genital or anal trauma
9) Sexually transmitted disease
10) Urinary tract infection

Long-term consequences of sexual abuse may include:

1) Delinquency
2) Drug abuse

3) Poor heterosexual relations
4) Prostitution
5) Sexual promiscuity
6) Guilt
7) Shame
8) Depression
9) Social Withdrawal
10) Emotional scarring into adulthood

Four adjustment patterns in response to sexual abuse include (1) avoidance; (2) repetition; (3) identification; and (4) integration. Psychological conflicts and stress associated with sexual abuse can be converted to physical symptoms.

Further challenging your medical acumen is the cultural/political climate surrounding sexual abuse, with one extreme summarily denying the self reports of children and the other extreme generating great alarm about child protection. There is no substitute for a balanced, objective, thorough, and sensitive medical examination.

SECTION III

DEVELOPMENTAL STAGES

CHAPTER 16

INFANCY:
WELCOME TO
OUR PLANET

Waldo made it. Nine of a thousand new borns had not. He had thought being born in the United States would have increased his chances for survival. After all, America is the wealthiest nation on the planet. We've put men on the moon, have an on-going affair with physical fitness, and have been "high tech-ing" our way into history. So how come we have such a high infant mortality rate? (Only 19 other countries in the world are worse!) Have some of our national priorities run amok?

Waldo didn't have time for casual conversation. Nine months in the womb wasn't long to get ready for the world "out there." Fortunately, he was healthy. But his journey down the birth canal had had its painful moments. He had heard horror stories of infancy, that period of life from his canal trip to two years of age. Infancy is the most dangerous time of any age: 5.5 deaths per thousand births in the first month alone! Baby's first trip is not a piece of cake.

Imagine what Waldo might have said, if he could speak, upon his arrival:

> "Who turned on the lights?!"
> "I'm hungry!"
> "Turn up the heat!"
> "Who's the big lug who just hit me on the butt?!"
> "I'm homesick already!"

Ah, to be a newborn again.

Fortunately Waldo's body was well prepared for his debut on this planet: His aorta diverted blood flow to his lungs, the alveoli filled with air and inflated his previously collapsed lungs, and the amniotic fluid which had cradled him in his fetal life became quickly absorbed into his lymphatic system. Renal function refines, kidneys increase their capability to concentrate or dilute urine (as any diaper service can testify), and eyesight improves from 2/150 at birth to 20/40 at year two of life. The most rapid growth occurs in the central nervous system, with the brain growing to 90% of its adult size in the first year. The length of Waldo's head is about a fourth of the size of his body! How would you like to have similar proportions? With your overall size right now, your head would be the size of a beach ball!

Following his birth, Waldo mused about his existence and his maternal care:

"Thank goodness Mom was mellow during my time inside. The kid in the next incubator had a mother who was really nervous, didn't eat nutritiously, and was depressed to the point that she was on medication. This kid was born prematurely, still can't sleep well, is irritable and hyperactive. The doctor said her mother's protein deficiency affected the baby's brain size and weight."

Prematurity, one of the health challenges neonates face, is defined as gestation of less than 34 weeks or birth weight under 2500 grams; it occurs in about 7% of all births. Prematurity puts the infant at greater risk for a variety of problems, including:

> Behavioral and emotional problems
> Mental retardation
> Dyslexia as well as other learning problems
> Child abuse

Life on the outside has its abrupt challenges for parents, too. One third to one half of mothers, for example, develop **postpartum depression** resulting from not only the abrupt hormone shifts within Mom, but also the significant stress surrounding child birth. Not only are physical demands placed on the new mother, with accompanying sleep deprivation and fatigue, but also the personal challenges of increased responsibility in caring for another separate (but markedly dependent) human being. An awesome mission indeed. This postpartum depression can be prolonged by a lack of social support from husband, family and friends, as well as from the mother being ill-prepared in terms of what to expect and what to do regarding the care and feeding of a newborn.

At birth the primary psychological challenge for the parents is to establish an intimate **bonding** or attachment with the infant. Failure to do so results in some significant physical and psychological consequences, including:

> Poor health and failure to thrive
> Developmental retardation
> Higher death rates in spite of adequate physical care.

Harry Harlow, a pioneering experimental psychologist, demonstrated the non-negotiable need for physical contact between mother and infant monkeys "or else:" i.e., significant impairment of social skills etc. Psychiatrist Rene Spitz, in his classic research at the University of Colorado and in Israeli kibbutzim, documented that human infants without responsive mothers develop severe problems and simply fail to thrive, "wilting on the vine." These infants died even in the presence of sanitary care that met all of their physical needs: They were fed regularly by bottles, had their diapers changed on schedule, etc. but did not have the hugs and touching which literally keep us alive.

And what of Waldo, our newborn? What can we expect of him? From a **physical** standpoint, he's quite a marvel to observe:

"Who made that sudden noise?"
> his body seems to say, as he jerks to attention, eyes wide, body rigid and mobilized in a startle response to a sharp noise (i.e., **Moro's reflex**).

"Give me five!"
> his grasp seems to communicate, as he clutches onto your finger with such strength that you can lift his body in the air (i.e., **palmar grasp reflex**).

"Your finger tickles!"
> he seems to gurgle, as his foot curls in response to you running your index finger down the length of the underside of his foot (i.e., **Babinski's sign**).

"Rub my lips!"
> His facial gestures seem to say, as he demonstrates a **sucking reflex** when you touch his mouth.

His sensory abilities, even at birth, have developed to the point that he can:

Discriminate sounds
Taste the difference between sweet and sour solutions
Make sounds reflecting his differing emotional states
Visually prefer more complex than simple patterns (e.g., magazine pictures
  and print preferred to simple lines).

Social/psychological development is equally impressive in the infant. Most parents note the initial ear-to-ear **smile** of their newborn, a smile that "obviously" means that she recognizes them as parents of the year! Well, not quite. For the first few weeks at least, this smile is simply a physical reflex. Later it contains some social meaning for the infant, e.g., "Hi Mom and Dad! How about an oil change?"

In about a half a year following birth, the infant's social awareness has matured to the point that she recognizes strangers and may cry and cling to her caretaker when a nonfamiliar face approaches. It makes sense that infants exposed to a number of caretakers demonstrate less **stranger anxiety** than those raised by only one parent.

And development continues! Within two brief years, a tiny organism who lives to drink, eat, wet and sleep becomes transformed into a walking, talking person with a mind of her own who is socially, emotionally and intellectually connected to the world of people and objects outside herself. She has begun to work in symbols, including the development of language, and has moved toward constructing a world of permanent objects apart from her own sense of self. She has started the rudiments of logical thinking, a primitive forerunner of more sophisticated reasoning that will characterize her later years.

But in our interest to sketch some characteristics of infancy, we lost Waldo, whom we left complaining about the heat, lights, and other sensory surprises in his new home. We've invited several consultants to observe him and make observations about what issues loom most significant at this level of development.

Dr. Freud, a word of explanation please!

"This *kinder* demonstrates, by his sucking reflex, his putting anything he can into his mouth, and his obvious pleasure with his bottle and mother's breast that his primary source of pleasure and gratification is his mouth. At this stage of development, he's an **oral** kind of guy!"

"Sigmund, although you make interesting points, I think we need to emphasize that the key issue in this baby's development, at least for his first year, is the establishment of a sense of **trust,**" interrupts Erik Erikson. "In order for Waldo to develop trust, he must develop the expectation that his basic needs will be fulfilled and that he can rely on his caregivers to respond to his signals in a reasonably consistent manner." Erikson continues, "From Waldo's 15 months to about two and a half years, he struggles with the conflicts of **autonomy vs. shame and doubt,** wrestling with his desires for independence from parental control. He achieves this autonomy when he is in control of his impulses and has achieved a sense of separateness from his mother."

"And what if I don't achieve this autonomy?" Waldo thinks to himself.

"Then," anticipates Erikson, who was somewhat of a mind-reader, "Waldo will feel that the world looks down on him and he will therefore experience a sense of shame."

"You're stealing my thunder, Erik!" steams Freud. "These toddler years are best described by my **anal stage** of development. It's a time when Waldo will arm wrestle with parents about toilet training, flexing the ol' sphincter muscle and letting them know whose in charge!"

"Don't forget his intellectual development!" chimes in Jean Piaget. In this young man's first two years of life, a time I call his **sensorimotor state,** he needs to learn how to understand and **assimilate** the stimuli in his environment as well as **accommodate** or alter his behavior in response to new stimulation. If all goes well, he'll develop the capacity to form an internal representation of an object, even when the object is taken from his view (**object constancy**)."

"Oh, Jean," sighed Freud, "you always were more 'in your head.' This next chapter gets us into some stimulating sexual stuff.

> So loosen up!
> Go with the flow!
> Out with the anal
> And let yourself grow!"

SUMMARY AND KEY POINTS

Babies are extremely vulnerable, both physically and socially. At birth, weighing in at an average of 7½ pounds and 20 inches in height, their senses are bombarded by the harshly stimulating environment outside the womb.

Healthy Moms help with this adjustment, giving their babies a head start with **in utero** balanced nutrition, stable emotions, and nontoxic chemicals circulating throughout the infants' systems.

Health challenges do occur:

1) The U.S. infant mortality rate is 9.2 per 1000 births.
2) Prematurity increases the risk for behavioral, emotional, intellectual/learning, and abuse problems.
3) Some mothers' postpartum blues and depression affect their ability to care for newborns.
4) Inadequate bonding and deficient physical/emotional nurturing from caretakers negatively impact the normal development of infants.

Impressive **physical** and **social/psychological development** occur over the first two years of life. Key developmental milestones include:

1) Oral and Anal Stages of Development (Freud)
2) The establishment of Trust vs. Mistrust and Autonomy vs. Shame and Doubt (Erikson)
3) Sensorimotor Stage: Cognitive assimilation and accommodation (Piaget)

CHAPTER 17

CHILDHOOD: THE WONDER YEARS

The joy of life danced in her eyes as she readied herself to race in the Whittier second grade 50 yard dash. She could barely contain herself, along with her two dozen classmates. They squirmed and jumped around, ebbing and flowing over the starting line, waiting for their teacher to blow the whistle to begin the race.

Such unbridled enthusiasm did not remain unchecked for long, however, as the shrill voice of Mildred the Mauler, better know as "The Teacher," rapidly enforced the social order.

"There will be no racing until we all line up in a single line . . . QUIETLY!" she ordered.

And they did. And my daughter did. Eyes downcast, spirit bruised but not broken, she assumed the demeanor of a miniature athlete doing a job . . . rather than a child reveling in the race of life. A bittersweet vignette . . . illustrating this magic time of childhood, the Wonder Years . . . from which we all must move . . . and grow up.

Childhood is the ten-year period of life between infancy and adolescence that most of us would love to occupy forever. The Wonder Years . . . a time of imaginary playmates, a time for parallel play with peers, a time for learning how to relate competently with colleagues of the same sex (the dating games will come later).

Freud sees later childhood as a **Latency period,** a time when sexual energy and sexual conflicts lie dormant. He does spend considerable time discussing very early childhood and the **Phallic stage.** This period involves struggling with the infamous **Oedipus/Electra complex** wherein the child competes with the opposite sex parent for the sexual attentions of the same sex parent.

Erikson describes childhood as characterized by stages of **initiative vs. guilt** (early childhood) and **industry vs. inferiority** (later childhood). He sees childhood as a time for carving one's own place in the world, making one's presence felt, and being "at risk" for being punished if one's behavior does not comply with the rules of society. During these times the child begins to discover that freedom involves responsibility, that her rights end where another person's nose begins. Her formation of a conscience is virtually complete. She identifies with parents, teachers, and authority figures, eagerly "toeing the line" to please. Parents love this age, for they become Mr. and Mrs. Wizard, the child's best friends, and the focus of boundless, unconditional love. Later, however, the child shifts her focus to peers and the outside world, moving her parents to the background and to a less obvious position of influence. It would be a mistake, however, to assume that parents no longer hold a critical posture of influence; their impact simply becomes less overt and obvious. For some parents, however, it seems that the powerful and sometimes heavy responsibilities of parenthood last forever.

Although the changes occurring during this period are not as dramatic as those of the preceding and succeeding periods, they are nonetheless profound and varied. The two-year-old has achieved a functional degree of maturation of all body systems. During childhood, these systems become increasingly more effective and efficient. This is especially true for the neurological and the **musculoskeletal systems.**

The toddler runs insecurely, but by the end of childhood she has developed a high degree of strength, coordination, and control. Her legs, which are bowlegged up to age two, become knock-kneed until she is twelve. But she can run the race, sensitive to her increasing mastery of more complex movements and games of coordination and skill. During this developmental period, however, sensory-motor coordination is highly variable among children and can be a double-edged sword: a source of satisfaction and pride as well as the vehicle for embarrassment and self-consciousness.

Neurological development is equally impressive. The child's brain grows to 96% of its adult size by the age of twelve. The increased physiological maturity of the central nervous system permits regulation of all major human functions from social skills to bowel and bladder control. In terms of the latter, most children are toilet trained early in their third year, although nighttime wetting can persist through the fifth year in 10% to 15% of children.

Cognitive development in the school-aged child is described by Piaget as in the stage of **concrete operation** until his early teens. In this stage, the child acquires his capacity for logical thought, i.e., for abstracting common elements from different objects. Pure abstract discussions and changing one's mind (i.e., reversibility of thinking) are still difficult. Some will never learn to change their minds. . . and so they become clerics, doctors, or politicians.

Language development explodes in early childhood, with the typical two-year-old learning 200 words (including amazing variations of the work, "NO!"), the three-year-old mastering 500 words, and the four-year-old speaking with a 1500 word vocabulary. By then, the verbal horse is out of the barn, as the child takes off running across the fields of expressive communication!

Sensory development, including vision and hearing, are mature by school age, but defects in these modalities can be harmful if not devastating, especially because sensory/perceptual deficiencies can be initially difficult to detect. The child who needs glasses or is hearing impaired may not complain because he has never known anything different. Early screening for sensory/perceptual problems is therefore imperative. It is a tragedy indeed when a child is labeled as a "slow learner" when, in fact, she cannot read the writing on the blackboard because of poor vision or cannot hear some of the lecture because of an auditory impairment.

In addition to sensory screening for vision and hearing, other parts of the medical examination for this age group routinely include:

1) Measuring height, weight, and head circumference (plotting them on a developmental graph)
2) Checking blood pressure
3) Hematocrit or hemoglobin
4) Immunizations
5) Urinalysis
6) Tuberculin Test
7) General physical examination
8) Developmental/behavioral assessment, including intelligence evaluation:
    a) Preschoolers—developmental inventory
    b) Older children—group administered standardized tests such as the Iowa Test of Basic Skills or individually administered intelligence tests such as the Wechsler Tests of Intelligence or the Peabody Picture Vocabulary Test).
9) Consultation with teachers, counselors, or other school staff regarding significant medical, learning or peer problems. Given that most children spend close to 40 hours a week in school, adequate medical care would require a viable, working relationship between yourself and the child's educators.

Learning handicaps are by no means rare, as mental retardation occurs in 3% of the children, and learning disabilities involve another 3% to 15% of the school population in the U.S. Early recognition and intervention are essential in remedying these problems, because "if Johnny can't read" etc., he has a major hurdle to overcome in achieving much academic success or feeling very good about himself.

Childhood is a vulnerable time for kids. The leading cause of death is **accidents,** including poisoning. Age three is the most dangerous time for poisoning as well as for child abuse. **Malignant tumors,** surprisingly, rank second. **Minor infections** are common, especially when children are brought together in school to "share their bugs." On the average, children experience six to seven "colds" a year, with their parents not far behind, with the latter's immunosuppression system already having a head start. It ain't all fun being a kid . . . particularly if you're not healthy . . . and have an occasional adult on your case!

SUMMARY AND KEY CONCEPTS

The Wonder Years . . . a time described by:

Freud as a **latency period** wherein sexual issues lie somewhat dormant. Freud does emphasize the very early childhood period (i.e., **phallic stage**), the time in which the child wrestles with love-competition feelings toward parents (Oedipus/Electra Complex).

Erikson would partially dispute Freud's impression of late childhood inactivity. He labels this period as a stage of **industry vs. inferiority,** a time for a child establishing a sense of competence in a world of his peers.

Piaget describes later childhood as a time for **concrete operations,** wherein logical reasoning begins to establish itself.

Major advances in the child's **musculoskeletal** and **neurological** systems occur, including escalating **language/communication** development. Medical evaluation needs to include, along with a **general physical** examination, a sensitivity toward **visual/hearing** problems and a **developmental/behavioral** assessment, including a general **intellectual** assessment. And don't forget about her **school.** It's a major player in her healthcare.

Beyond the biomedical, however, there is, during childhood, the blossoming of a child . . . wonderful . . . and wondering.

CHAPTER 18

ADOLESCENCE: TAMING THE TASMANIAN DEVIL

A frustrated parent once said that the leading cause of adult alcoholism is teenagers. A second parent discussed his newest "get rich quick" scheme called "swap-a-teen." Each couple within the group would exchange among themselves each others' kids, waiting until each grew weary of one another, and then they would switch again. You would almost think that these parents viewed their adolescents as uncontrolled creatures from another world . . . the Bugs Bunny comic book terrors-of-the-universe Tasmanian devils! Parents don't, but jokes and stories abound about the teenage years, stories that reflect the emotional, physical and behavioral dilemmas encountered by these child/adult hybrids.

Over a cup of coffee, a psychologist friend confided that he has developed a theory of teenagers that "cuts through" a lot of academic philosophizing. He calls it the "Entomological Theory of Adolescence." In brief, he postulated that around the age of twelve or thirteen, human young became exquisitely vulnerable to a certain insect, *Obnoxious Terribilis,* which crawls up their alimentary canal and creates all sorts of behavior problems: snarling at siblings, rebelling against rules, pouncing on parents, dabbling in drugs, fixation with phoning, sensory saturation with sights and sounds, and experimenting with sex in its various shapes and sizes. When the host reaches twenty, the bug exits, nevermore to return. This theory, if accepted, may set off a feverish search for an over-the-counter drug that will kill the little buggers (the insects, not the teenagers).

In a less profane spirit, adolescence is the time of life between twelve and twenty when the child transforms into an adult. The metamorphosis starts with a microscopic biochemical shift in the hypothalamus of a lovable child and ends with a full-grown, psychologically intact adult. This process is neither calm nor orderly, does not follow a predictable timetable, is not the same for everyone, but does involve predictable and natural emotional upheaval. According to Anna Freud, "Adolescence is by its very nature an interruption of peaceful growth; the upholding of a steady equilibrium during the adolescent process is in itself abnormal." Who would argue with Freud's daughter?!

A current expert on adolescent development, my wife (who also is a middle school counselor), observes that teenagers are sometimes like two-year-olds, but with active hormones and wheels. This tongue-in-cheek observation actually has some research support, as the onset of puberty is apparently due to a decrease in the sensitivity of the hypothalamus to circulating sex steroids. That is, the hypothalamic-pituitary secretions of gonadal-stimulating hormones continues in the presence of increasing levels of sex hormones, which would previously have suppressed this secretion. The result is greater levels of ovarian and testicular hormones secreted in response to higher levels of gonadotropins. This in turn leads both to sexual maturation and rapid growth in physical size and strength. The profound psychological changes that occur at this time are largely the result of these physical changes. If there is a direct effect of the sex hormones on the brain, as is generally assumed, it requires a certain neurological maturation, because precocious puberty does not lead to heightened sexual interest. For sex hormones to stimulate sexual interest, the brain needs to reach a certain level of maturity. Or less pedantically, the above physiological findings would tend to support the observation that most adolescence have "sex on the brain."

Stages of Adolescence

Psychologically, adolescence is divided into early, middle and late periods. With most physical characteristics, girls generally mature about two years before boys. The tasks of **early adolescence** (11 to 14 years), a stage marked by dramatic endocrine changes, are awareness and acceptance of **sexual maturation** and the beginnings of a drive towards **emancipation from the parents.** The family, however, is still the primary focus. This early period is characterized by a heightened **sensitivity to the opinions of peers.** If some **body image** challenges occur (such as slightness of build, obesity, acne, or late breast development), emotional fallout may result. Such issues may appear insignificant to the examining physician, but be assured that they loom as a "big deal" to the anxious adolescent.

In **middle adolescence** (14 to 17 years), the key conflict surrounds the struggle for independence from parental control. The peer group becomes the dominant influence, with gender roles and sexual identity, body image, and popularity occupying center stage in the teenager's life. By this time, most girls have reached menarche. Visions of the opposite sex dance in their heads, accompanied by fantasies probably warped by television and locker room exaggeration.

In **late adolescence** (17 to 20 years), crystallization of a stable identity occurs along with the establishment of career, marriage, and life philosophy goals. Any of these stages may be delayed or thwarted by illness or adverse life situations. They may also be reached prematurely, as in the case of the school dropout, early marriage, or early childbearing. In most persons, this period marks the development of a moral and ethical sense, sometimes reflected in humanitarian concerns. The key developmental challenge according to Erikson is **identity vs. role confusion,** i.e., sorting out one's own unique identity in contrast to going along with the crowd.

Phil Mohan, senior developmental psychologist at the University of Idaho, has summarized adolescents' three most important needs as follows:

1) Centrality of sex, including concerns about:
   a) Body image
   b) Being sexually active, petting, pregnancy, abortion
   c) Masturbation
   d) Sexual maturation: being an "early developer" or "late bloomer"
2) Drive for independence
   For example, finances are seen as a way to get out of the house, away from the folks, and live on one's own.
3) Quest for Identity
   a) Adolescence is a period of "temporary insanity" that everyone goes through in their normal development.
   b) In order to develop an internal sense of self, active experimentation with various "looks" occurs. The teenager may shock you with his orange Mohawk haircut and "grunge" look, but his message generally is, "Don't pay attention to the obvious. Look inside. Look at who I really am."
   c) Peer group rules!
   d) Conflict and crisis are **necessary** for a viable identity quest; they are also cognitively stimulating.
   e) Erikson: Two ingredients are necessary for the resolution of the **identity vs. role confusion** conflict:
      (1) Crisis: the active exploration of identities and values.
      (2) Commitment: action/behavior in response to these values.

From a medical viewpoint, adolescence is a time of relatively good health. Representative problems that you will undoubtably encounter include:

1) Sexually related problems, including teenage pregnancies, abortion inquiries, birth control counseling, and socially transmitted diseases
2) Substance abuse, including alcohol and tobacco
3) Accidents
4) Suicides
5) Communication/interpersonal problems with parents

Access to medical care is a particular challenge for this age group, as they generally don't trust "the older generation," which includes doctors. Doctors typically don't like teenage patients, as witnessed by the earlier sample of "jokes" about adolescents in this chapter. Adolescent patients are concerned about confidentiality, because they have a "push me - pull you" attitude toward parents and parental surrogates (i.e., "I want to do this, I think, but I want you to say 'no' so I can't," etc.). Bathed in such emotional confusion, teenagers present a significant challenge, both professionally and personally, to the busy Doc with a roomful of "easy" patients. But they're worth it! Where else can you find such a whirling dervish of nervous energy who is fiercely dedicated to making the world a better place . . . if only he can pass geometry and get a date with the only girl he will ever love!

SUMMARY AND KEY CONCEPTS

Adolescence, the period described by many as **developmental insanity,** has become the butt of jokes, the ultimate challenge for parents, and a cross to bear for many doctors. Consider a lighter perspective toward teenagers. Don't take their external appearances and mannerisms as valid indices of who they really are, i.e., scared kids on an emotional roller coaster ride to adulthood. They don't bite . . . most of the time.

This period of "reversible brain damage," as Dr. Bill Cosby describes it, is divided into **early, middle** and **late** periods, each with its biological and psychological markers. But don't sweat the details. Try to capture the spirit of what these folks go through. After all, you were there once! (You obviously are not still there, or you would have stopped reading this chapter and would be out skateboarding by now.)

Three **major issues** are confronted in adolescence:

1) Sex
2) Independence
3) Identity.

That's enough to keep anyone busy. So when you see teenagers in your office, hang loose. They have got a lot on their mind!

CHAPTER 19

YOUNG ADULTHOOD: STRETCHING FOR THE BRASS RING

Ben Bandaid shook his head as he walked from class. His appearance in Chapter 4 as an example of psychoanalytic principles had been an ego boost, but he continued to struggle with all the stress he was experiencing in medical school. He was a member of the "Twenty-Thirty Somethings" generation, and young adulthood was not a cakewalk. When he read Freud, he got the impression that all important developments within the human psyche had occurred by the time he was five years old. Even if he had not paid all his developmental dues by five, certainly after all the adolescent turmoil (e.g., *Obnoxious Terribilis,* sex, **identity** vs. role confusion, sex, movement toward **independence** from parental control, and **sex**), Ben could now rest on his laurels and coast through adult life. Not!

Physically, Ben knew that this time of life was about as good as it gets. Most everything in his body worked, and worked rather well: His bod was strong, supple, vigorous, and hard. Just like the magazine ads said. Internally, his heart, lungs and other body systems functioned as finely honed machines, cruising through aerobics, biking and hiking briskly through life, disgesting pizza without a care about cholesterol . . . bullet proof . . . at least for awhile. Hey, why not enjoy! There was certainly no hurry in becoming a representative of the next two chapters (i.e., middle age and old age). Ben wanted to revel in the sunshine for awhile, but some developmental agenda were impacting his reveling:

1) In adolescence he had broken away from his nuclear family, establishing a life of his own along with his own **autonomy.** He had moved out of his family's home before med school and it felt good. But he missed his folks and had to settle for their emotional support being "long distance." There was an invigorating challenge about taking care of himself and his daily needs,

including his finances, but the loneliness took some getting use to (as well as the 18% interest on **his** credit cards, which were now in **his** name). But he was off on his personal and vocational quests, carving out a niche for himself.

2) He now needed more than a sense of his own identity. He was searching for special relationships. He had read that Erikson talks about this time of life being characterized by the pull between establishing **intimacy vs. isolation.** This was to be his time for establishing intimate relationships.

Intimate relationships . . . Peggy Sue . . . and the *m* word—**marriage.** Awesome and scary, this marriage thing . . . with its initial honeymoon phase, then periods of disenchantment, renewed commitments, or possibly divorce. Ben, being the logical sort, started sifting out some of the advantages of marital bliss:

Sex without AIDS. (Ain't he the romantic one, this hormone-
hampered hypothalamic hunk!)

Two can live cheaper than one. (So he's not an economist!).

Two can get more work done than one. (He's clearly an optimist!).

Greater happiness and personal satisfaction

In combing through his memories of his undergraduate Marriage and Family class, Ben recalled earlier research studies indicating that married people report greater happiness and satisfaction than single, divorced or widowed folks. More recent studies have narrowed this gap: people who have never married (especially men) report greater happiness, while married people (especially women) say they are less happy and content than single people.

For Ben (and for many of us), intimate relationships and the "love potion" formula are tough to figure out: They're powerful and complex critters that don't seem to lend themselves easily to chemical or scientific analysis.

Oops! Ben forgot an important characteristic of marriage: It generally creates an orderly environment for raising kids.

3) Beginning a family . . . kids already! Whoa! This young adulthood snowball was beginning to accelerate way too quickly. "**Parenthood!**" Ben muttered. "I'm not even engaged yet!"

The shift from being "two" to being "three" (i.e., couplehood to family) involves a major shift in values, attitudes, and roles. Ben was still stretching to move from thinking about "two" instead of "one!"

"Peggy Sue and Tyler too," thought Ben. The prospect of a wife and now a child put him more in a "family way" than he was initially comfortable in accepting. Ben's ability to make the personal and interpersonal transitions from self, to couple, to family will have a marked impact on the quality of his relationships with his future wife and children.

As these transitions occur, predictable crises develop. Peggy Sue may present symptoms of fatigue, sleep problems, and emotional distress. Ben may appear bothered more by changes in plans, financial concerns, and interference of in-laws. In general, couples with young children experience more stress than any other developmental group. For both parents, satisfaction ratings tend to drop and remain at a less passionate plateau until the children leave home. Factors that can increase the odds for satisfaction and happiness during this period include:

Wanting children, proactively seeking their presence in one's life

Ability to draw on outside resources for time, money, and energy

The couple knowing each other for some time

Having a firm sense of independence as a couple

One of the primary sources of conflict for married couples involves their differences in child-rearing beliefs.

4) Launching a meaningful **career** that dovetails with one's identity is a major issue in this stage of development. One traditional marker of adulthood in our culture is getting a job, although such a venture can often be delayed by continued training and education. We don't have to remind you that work during this developmental period is the focus of enormous investments of time, energy, and commitment. As you, like Ben, articulate a work role, such a role adds to and helps resolve identity issues that have continued from adolescence. From now on until retirement, there will be an ongoing interaction between family and work that can cut two ways: The work-family dynamic can result in heightened conflict or produce increased satisfaction.

The job-launching process is often difficult, with the first year on a job being a critical time indeed! As the new kids on the employment block, we can go through somewhat of an initiation rite. As new cogs in a working wheel, Ben and Peggy Sue must fact fears about their competence and self-worth. Us too!

Choosing a job or picking the "right" profession appears dependent upon a variety of factors:

Intelligence and aptitudes

Educational background

Interests

Work history

Socioeconomic status

Ethnic origin

Sex

Race

Physical health

Job availability

This list gives you a flavor of the variables that interact with one another and that establish our range of occupational choices.

Once initiated into a particular work arena, we confront some realities that are often harsh. There may be significant inconsistencies between our expectations and the actual demands of the job. For example, Peggy Sue's work role needs to become a part of her sense of self. For most of us, our work is an extension of ourselves. If our work does not fit with our perceptions of ourselves, obvious conflicts arise. Work satisfaction and adjustment appear related to such factors as:

Job description permitting a worker to function in her desired role

Ability of the job to use a worker's ability and training

Worker's reaction to authority (e.g., supervision, orders, etc.)
Incentives (e.g., pay increases, promotions, etc.)

Work stress and conflicts generate medical problems. Unemployment, for example, can take a chunk out of a person's self-worth and push him out of the mainstream of society. "Languishing in the unemployment line" can increase a person's risk for drug abuse, alcoholism, marital stress, sexual dysfunction, and psychosomatic illness. On the other extreme, excessive involvement in work and joining the ranks of the workaholic can create marked wear and tear on the worker, including symptoms characteristic of Type A behavior which is frequently associated with the development of heart disease (Remember our chapter on stress, p.44?).

As you can probably personally attest (Ben and Peggy Sue certainly can!), the young adulthood period (20 to 40 years of age) is not, in fact, bulletproof. Good health is generally the rule. However, more than half of all disabling injuries occur before the age of 35. Challenges to health include:

Stress and stress-related pathology
Accidents
Drug and alcohol use
Sexually related dysfunction and disease

Common behavioral risk factors predicting poor health include:

Drinking and driving
Heavy drinking
"Couch potato" lifestyle
Obesity
Smoking
Hypertension

Lifestyle patterns laid down in adolescence and young adulthood typically provide the templates for later health as well as for later pathology. For example, some of the degenerative seeds of coronary heart disease have already been sewn in early adulthood. You, as a physician, can be a major player in preventing such disease development. By encouraging healthy lifestyles, in addition to treating specific disorders themselves, you can strike a blow for better health habits . . . and better health! A medical commitment to primary prevention programs e.g., weight control, healthy diet, proper exercise, sensible alcohol intake, reduction in smoking, etc.) can indeed be a solid medical investment in your patient's future. Ben, bring on those exercise bikes!

SUMMARY AND KEY CONCEPTS

Ben Bandaid is back again, and this time as a young adult dealing with the following developmental agenda:

1) Establishing **autonomy** apart from his nuclear family
2) Wrestling with the issues of **intimacy vs. isolation** (Erikson)
3) Pondering **parenthood** and **family**
4) Launching a **career**

In this chapter we discussed challenges and risk factors to health and made a passionate pitch for lifestyles that retard or prevent illness.

CHAPTER 20

MIDDLE AGE:
"#@*&%$!!@#!*&%^!"

Cuss words! It ain't easy having one foot on the dock and the other on the boat. The energized vessel of youth begins to gradually pull away, while our bodies seem anchored in the aging process, creaking and groaning from the storms of stress and the tempests of time. Whoa! Is there any doubt about what stage of life this author is in! And I did not look forward one bit to writing this chapter . . . I'd rather be in denial!

Physically, some sobering changes have inexorably occurred. A half dozen exercise machines and several thousand dollars later, I stand convinced that my days for becoming an Olympic athlete are numbered . . . painfully numbered. Muscles don't work as well, and when they do, the ol' coordination ain't what it used to be, and pain is most always a companion.

You're thinking, "Am I going to have to listen to some old fart complain *ad nauseam* about his aches and pains? I've got gross anatomy to study!"

But that's what I'm talking about. . . gross anatomy! **Real** gross anatomy! Well, actually it isn't that bad, but middle-aged patients like me are going to be darkening your office doorstep with our complaints, so cinch up and get prepared!

Here are some of the "biological facts" about these middle years you and your patients must contend with (sounds like a cadaver's worst nightmare):

Decrease in muscle mass

Presbyopia (decreased near-focusing ability due to aging)

Compromise in hormone production resulting in female and male menopause.
  For men, the changes are primarily psychological, although a flabby body, getting winded while jogging to the refrigerator, and a penis that takes naps during intercourse do not help.

For women, menopause includes the ending of menstruation as a result of a decrease of estrogen production. Although some may experience anxiety and depression, most women go through this change relatively free of symptoms.
Increased osteoporosis
Decreased brain weight, the loss of 50,000 neurons a day, resulting in reduced memory and overall cognitive functioning
The replacement function of cells falls behind
Loss of skin elasticity
Hair loss
Candlelight becomes necessary to improve one's body image

Are we having fun yet?

Given these failing physical changes, a physician can expect to see a greater incidence of such problems as:

> Hypertension
> Diabetes
> Cardiac problems
> Chronic obstructive pulmonary disease
> Strokes
> Cancer
> Cirrhosis of the liver
> Compulsive need to make lists of middle age diseases

And there is more! Additional cognitive/behavioral changes challenge the middle aged. Erikson notes that the intimacy vs. isolation conflicts of early adulthood blend into **generativity vs. stagnation** in mature adulthood. Generativity refers not only to coming to terms with one's children who are preparing to leave home, but also with one's parents, who may be requiring more care. Mature adults receive challenges from the generations on either side of them. Work and career changes also are in flux, cresting for many, wilting for some. Brass rings can be tarnishing, sacred cows no longer give milk, and the power surge up the corporate ladder begins to short out.

Oh, great! Not only do our bodies fall apart and we're threatened with stagnating, but there is yet another whole list of developmental tasks to accomplish!

1) **The care and feeding of adolescent children.** It's common knowledge that insanity is inherited. (We get if from our kids!) As middle-aged parents observe their brain cells diminish, their teenagers struggle with separation from family and formation of their own individual identities. In the process, they may challenge parental values, authority battles may ensue, and power struggles between parent and adolescent (i.e., child-captured-in-adult-body) may abound. At some point, **both** teenagers **and** parents may attempt to run away from home. Although we tease and joke about wanting the kids to be on their own, their absence can leave some mighty large shoes to fill.

The empty nest syndrome, the result of the kids flying the coop, can mark a critical period in a middle-aged person's life. Traditionally, women have been described as reacting to this time with depression and despair, but current research suggests that the majority of mothers see this launching as a time of relief that often leads to an increase in both personal and marital satisfaction. Fathers don't necessarily have an easy time seeing their kids leave either. After all, why do most fathers bust their buns bringing home the bacon, if the youngsters are not there to eat it? Men get accused of living to work and relegating the raising of kids to "women's work." Bull. Mr. Moms abound. Nothing can light up the heart of a father any quicker or make life worth living any more than a hug from a daughter or a smile from a son. And you can take that opinion to the bank!

Lest you get too nostalgic, however, the empty nest frequently does not stay that empty. Grandkids come along. But before then, the original occupants may come back! Dr. Bill Cosby observes that human beings are the only species that allows their young to return home. Once out of school (a process that appears to be taking longer and longer), offspring are finding it increasingly more difficult to find jobs, particularly jobs that allow them to maintain a household on a single income. They can also become single parents, divorce early, or flounder in their ability to support themselves. A return to the nest is not problem free, as the children, who are not really children anymore, are put at risk in terms of remaining dependent and immature. Their parents can be deprived of the freedom to renew and update their relationship with each other and to explore their own personal development apart from being parents.

2) **The care and feeding of one's parents.** It seems that just about the time middle-aged persons have raised their kids, they have the opportunity to raise their parents. A role reversal occurs, requiring one to parent his parents. This switch in roles does not necessarily come easily, because feelings of frustration, anger, and resentment can characterize both generations as they struggle to relate to each other by means of new ground rules. Both generations can feel thrust onto a field of conflict which neither chooses: Generally older folks don't want to be taken care of, and the younger folks don't want to interfere with their parents' independence. Brother can argue with brother about the merits of Dad being maintained at home versus being moved into the progressive cycle of supervised (and eventually institutional) care. When a family experiences such wrenching dilemmas, your help (along with other health care professionals seasoned in dealing with the elderly and extended families) can be invaluable.

3) **Work.** By this time in a man's life, he has reached the peak of his career or is at the threshold of a new vocation. A woman, however, may just be warming up professionally. With the children's rearing well in tow, mom may be entering the job market. Although several decades have passed since the Women's Movement has legitimized female vocational ambitions outside the home, men and women still remain on different timetables regarding the work force. The middle-aged male is beginning to shift his vocational life into a

lower gear, while his wife is catching her second wind and is raring to go. Perhaps the nest is empty, additional money is needed for the kids' college, or she is experiencing her own personal and professional metamorphosis.

A note of disclaimer: The preceding remarks apply to the author's middle-age generation and the man-woman-family-work *Zeitgeist*. These attitudes, values and patterns may become completely out of date by the time you reach middle-age.

Wear and tear runs freely within the work environment, with stresses which include lack of promotion, low pay, office politics, shifting job descriptions, pressures to produce, split allegiances between home and job, and cutbacks or unemployment. In your office you can observe work stress revealing itself in such symptoms as

> Alcohol abuse
> Smoking
> High cholesterol
> Increased heart disease
> Depression
> Anxiety
> Vague somatic complaints with no
> demonstrable biological pathology

Burnout in the work place is as real a medical problem as a broken arm, but can prove even more handicapping. Classic stress induction parameters are in place: One's body's alarm reaction has transformed to a more long-term resistance response, which eventually involves most or all of the body systems. Exhaustion is predictable, disease producing and occasionally fatal. In Japan there is a specific phrase describing a person literally dying from overwork. Sometimes when a patient says, "My work is killing me," he literally may be correct!

4) **Midlife crisis.** A hateful word to me, as this time seems to have become synonymous with a forty-something man getting divorced, buying a red sports car, and racing down life's highway with his partially balding head being kissed by the balmy breezes . . . and the buxom blond slinking next to him. The forties can result in some dramatic changes in lifestyle, including reframing and updating key relationships, particularly with one's spouse, reshaping one's career, and learning how to dance with one's mortality. Although technically "successful," a person can experience the emptiness of some victories. The brass rings may look tarnished, and the golden idols may ring false and tinny. Unfulfilled dreams may appear as nightmares. One's life may feel unfulfilled and empty. As Shakespeare might say, "Life sucketh!" Yet this time need not be a trauma, as dancing with one's inner demons can leave one less tyrannized by inner conflicts, the arbitrary demands of others, and more accepting of oneself. As one of Jess Lair's first books exclaims, "I Ain't Much Baby, But I'm All I've Got!"

Earlier we detailed some of the physical symptoms of this stage in life. High-risk psychological challenges can include:

Depression
Alcohol abuse and dependence
Suicide

All of the preceding symptoms can be masked as the middle-aged patient sits at the end of your examining table.

Rancher Rick, a middle-aged man who rarely complains, looks at you through tired eyes and says, "Doc, I just can't seem to sleep! I ache all over. And I'm pooped all the time." His wife might haltingly add that Rick seems to be drinking too much, is worrying more about work, and avoids sexual intimacy because he has problems performing. Rick's eyes begin to tear, but only slightly, as he looks at his feet and says nothing. The diagnostic red flags are up. Be aware of their meaning.

It would be a mistake to leave you with only half of the story about middle age. There's some good news, too. While improving your relationship with your **body,** you become aware that:

- It's the only one you will be issued, and that's O.K.
- Sex becomes savored and sophisticated instead of slam-bam.
- Your appetite for big meals wanes but your waist line doesn't notice.
- Sleep seems less sacred and more illusive.
- It's possible to pull a muscle by combing your hair.

During middle age, you begin to become cozier with your **emotions,** observing that:

- Your feelings may not be in the majority, but that's O.K.
- You begin to revel in your inner world and like being you.
- Anger is a total waste of energy and time.
- Belly laughs have healing power.
- Machines and money are hard to cuddle with.
- The Marlboro Man must have been one lonely SOB.

Relationships with people take on a sense of greater importance as you notice that:

- Friends appreciate **you** instead of your trappings and trophies.
- Kicking ass and kissing ass are inappropriate uses of that anatomical part.
- Energy drainers and time wasters are quickly removed from your guest list.
- When you get an itch that is hard to scratch, you are less embarrassed to call for help.
- Kids bring the greatest joy and the deepest sorrow.
- Now you can reintroduce yourself to your spouse . . . and get more of it "right" this time!

Work during middle age can become transformed into a user-friendly endeavor as we learn that:

- Brass rings don't smell as sweet as roses.
- Money seems less important and more available.
- Few people want their jobs description, resumé and bank balance etched on their tomb stone.
- Nobody cares what we do on the job, unless we step on their toes, so we can really do what we think is best . . . and make a real positive difference in this world of ours.

The quest for making our lives count for something takes on a special sense of urgency during middle-age. Many search for meaning beyond the material, hounding heaven for answers, and sometimes discovering that God does not have to be Catholic . . . or Protestant . . . or Jewish . . . or Moslem . . . or male . . . or female . . . or a white-haired magician in the sky. We begin to appreciate the wisdom of Mark Twain, as he wryly observed that God made man into his image and likeness, and then man promptly returned the favor. In middle age, our vision quest becomes legitimized.

SUMMARY AND KEY CONCEPTS

Middle age is not terminal. It just feels that way sometimes. Physical deterioration has begun, but don't worry about memorizing the list of anatomical changes. Your middle-aged patients will refresh your memory soon enough. Care enough to listen beyond the organ recital to the rumblings in their spirit.

Erikson describes these developmental years from forty through the mid-sixties as characterized by the conflict of **generativity vs. stagnation.** Developmental tasks include:

1) The care and feeding of **children** and their leaving the nest
2) Coping with older **parents**
3) Evolution of one's vocation and **work**
4) **Midlife crisis**
5) Discovering the **good news** about middle age

See you there before you know it!

CHAPTER 21

OLD AGE: GOING GENTLY INTO THAT GOOD NIGHT

His bent eighty-seven-year old frame, his shuffling walk, and his cognitive slippage marked Grandpa Frank Seitz Senior as an old man, but he didn't believe it for a minute.

"Son," he said, "there's **old** people living at the Country Club (his term of affection for the Beaver Creek Respite Center for the Aged)." Then a twinkle rippled through his look. "Maybe that includes me, too."

Maybe. The book says sixty-five. That's when we are suppose to enter "Old Age." Dad doesn't think he's there yet. But he is there, from my perspective. This once independent, strong-minded German with a four-letter-work vocabulary that would make a longshoreman blush can no longer care for himself. He's changed with age, some normal changes and some pathological:

1) My father doesn't **hear** well now.

2) His failing **vision** is somewhat corrected by glasses . . . if he remembers where he's put them.

3) He's **shorter** and much **less muscular** than years ago when I tried to arm wrestle him . . . then, a futile act indeed.

4) He prefers Twinkies and donuts to the "four food groups" and a balanced diet. This, of course, creates **poor nutrition** and **digestive problems.**

5) He routinely denies "dunking donuts" but his **memory** serves him poorly. What he doesn't remember, he makes up and "fills in the blanks" (**confabulation**).

6) He sighs more now and **breathes shallow** breaths. His **heart** pumps less vigorously.

7) His **skin** is wrinkled, having lost its elasticity and no longer stretching over his once bulging muscles.

8) And the cradle of his mind has shrunk in size, his ventricles and cortical sulci yawn wider as his cerebral vessels become stingy in the amount of blood they transport to his **brain.**

Intellectual changes have resulted in significant cognitive decline. Such decline is more than the result of normal aging and is considered pathological. He is suffering from **dementia,** a disorder once referred to as senility, which describes cognitive impairment including such symptoms as:

1) **Memory dysfunction,** particularly immediate memory
> e.g., "Where did I put that @#&*!# newspaper!" which he just took from the doorstep and placed at the side of his chair.
2) Language disturbance (**aphasia**)
> e.g., "Could you hand me that 'thing-a-ma-jig [*pencil*]?"
3) Impaired ability to carry out certain movements in spite of intact motor function (**apraxia**).
> e.g., A retired mechanic asking, "How do you change this car tire?"
4) Failure to recognize or identify familiar objects in spite of intact sensory function (**agnosia**)
> e.g., Failure to recognize that a plastic plate cannot be placed on hot stove burner without the plate melting and creating a fire danger.
5) Disturbances in planning, organizing, sequencing, abstracting, etc. (**executive functioning**)
> e.g., A self-employed businessman who has done his own accounting for years now has problems balancing his checkbook.
6) Significant **impairment in social or occupational functioning**
> e.g., A former welder replies, "A can't find my tools, and when I do, I don't remember how to use them!"

Alzheimer's Disease is the best known in the dementia category, and has cognitive/behavioral characteristics similar to the six we've just mentioned. Alzheimer's has a distinctive pattern of neurophysiological pathology, but, unfortunately, such patterns are not definitively distinguishable without an autopsy.

The developmental challenge at this stage of life, according to Erikson, involves **ego integrity vs. despair.** On the one hand, a person can bask with pride in his sense of accomplishment or can languish in a tar pit of despair at his having "missed the mark." Dealing with major losses and coming to terms with the "wonders and the warts" of one's life represent the challenges of this developmental period. Successfully negotiating this final stage can find one the embodiment of Popeye the Sailor's epitaph, "I yam what I yam!" . . . and proud of it!

In addition to the physical and cognitive changes of old age, the elderly face psychological challenges. **Depression** is the most common mental health problem, involving about 15% of those over 65, with 3% of that number experiencing major depression. However, depression does not naturally accompany aging, although the numerous **losses** experienced by the elderly certainly put them at high risk for affective problems:

1) Loss through death or other means of one's spouse, family and friends
2) Deteriorating health
3) Retirement from one's vocation/job and the social, financial and personal support such a position provides
4) Loss of independence and sense of control, as one's body fails, one's mind falters, one's finances collapse, and one's social support system becomes dependent on institutions and agencies

Fortunately, geriatric depression is treatable with psychotherapy, medication, and Electroconvulsive Shock Therapy (ECT). As a postscript, ECT can be a remarkably effective therapeutic modality, contrary to *One Flew Over the Cuckoo's Nest* type of reputation, and can actually be safer for the elderly than some antidepressant drugs.

Suicide risk is higher for the elderly. Paradoxically, with the exception of organic brain dysfunction and depression, older people demonstrate less psychological symptomotology than their younger counterparts. Misuse of medications can also contaminate the older person's clinical picture, many times creating cognitive confusion that can be misdiagnosed as dementia. Similarly, depression can produce symptoms easily mistaken for cognitive impairment and dementia.

Such changes, both natural and pathological, accompany Grandpa Frank and others on their journeys through old age. But physical status or age is rarely the measure of a man . . . and chronological age is not necessarily the same thing as biological age nor an accurate predictor of health.

Not only Grandpa Frank is graying. So is America. The U.S. Census Bureau and the National Institute on Aging report that the number of Americans older than 85 will more than double in the next 25 years to 7 million people. Unfortunately, the "oldest old," as this group is known, may require massive amounts of expensive medical care. Of the 3 million Americans in this group, 30% have Alzheimer's disease and 24% of them live in nursing homes. The oldest old group is growing significantly faster than the elderly as a whole—who in turn are growing much faster than the entire population. The Census Bureau expect the 65-and-older age group, now 33 million, to exceed 53 million in 2020. With less than 13% of all Americans, this group consumed about one third of all health spending last year, approximately $330 billion of the nation's $1 trillion health bill.

Analysts have found a strong correlation between education and good health later in life. They are encouraged that 25% of the baby boom generation, born from 1946 to 1964, have college degrees, compared with less than 9 percent of today's 65-and-over population. These legions of baby boomers, blessed with good health from decades of proper diet and exercise, will be enjoying life well into their 90s. The National Institute on Aging predicts that medical breakthroughs will help postpone or prevent chronic disabling conditions among the elderly. For instance, drugs to control high blood pressure, treat cholesterol and relieve osteoporosis could keep millions of people out of nursing homes.

Some **behavioral strategies** also seem promising in dealing with the elderly:

1) Regular **physical activity** and exercise which can help with restful sleep, chronic aches and pains, muscle tone, and emotional distress

2) **Social support** from existing friends and family, as well as linking up with new souls who can be supportive (e.g., Adopt a Grandparent, Senior Centers, Humane Society, Rent-a-Rector etc.)

3) Proper **nutrition**

4) Reasonable and regular **medical examinations** for undiagnosed acute illness which the elderly so often attribute to "just getting old"

5) Making one's **life meaningful—now!** Like the Rene Spitz research with infants who perished without emotional nurturing (Infancy chapter, pp.104-105), old folks can wilt on the vine for similar reasons.

Old Age can be viewed in too dark of terms. If the biology of the elderly is given sole priority in geriatric medicine, along with the assumption that we all should live forever, there is risk that we can miss the forest for the trees . . . the splendor of experiencing the seasons of humanity, winter as well as spring. And there indeed is splendor in our later years. We need look no further than our family for the proof.

SUMMARY AND KEY CONCEPTS

In Old Age, **physical changes** abound:

1) Decline in hearing and vision
2) Reduction in height, weight, and muscle mass
3) Digestive problems
4) Decrease in cardiac output
5) Loss of skin's elasticity
6) Brain deterioration
    a) Physiological changes
    b) Cognitive changes, including memory deterioration
    c) Affective changes, particularly depression

Pathological conditions resulting from the preceding physiological changes, as well as from personal, family, social, and vocational changes:

1) Organic brain syndromes, including dementia and Alzheimer's disease
2) Depression and increased suicide risk

3) Medication-induced symptoms that mimic dementia-like cognitive impairment.

The elderly need not "go to seed" prematurely nor write their epitaph too early. Exercise, proper diet, nurturing relationships, and a deeply felt sense of self-worth can help move one out of the rocking chair and into a vital reality. Or as Grandpa Frank would say, "An 'old fart' is a terrible thing to waste."

CHAPTER 22

DYING AND DEATH: THE COCOON AND THE BUTTERFLY

Before the sophistry of technology, death was not regarded as an enemy. Healers were not expected to make their patients' "unharvestable" for the "Grim Reaper." Healers were considered fellow travelers on the journey of life, a journey that all expected to end sometime. That was before cosmetic ads, vitamins, and exercise machines implied a promise of everlasting youth. Voices in our Western culture, from poets and artists, from native American ancients, speak of "dying well." They speak of dying as a process as natural as being born, and that we are equipped to do both. They speak of death being a metamorphosis, like the butterfly shaking itself from it's cocoon. Unfortunately, few of us have beheld such a butterfly, a person who has cheated death, but we have heard stories. . . . Our science has not yet been able to put death and resurrection under a microscope, but we have heard of "near-death experiences" dramatically detailing a golden light and life beyond this vale of tears. We have heard the Bible speak of a God/man who broke the bonds of death. Most of us have not seen the butterfly. Do we dare believe it exists? You are in the business of dealing with dying. Perhaps it's time to dance with the doctrines of death. This chapter won't be able to do that for you, but hopefully we can raise some issues that will whet your appetite.

Knowing how to deal with dying and death implies that we know how to live. If you don't, how are you planning on preparing to treat vulnerable patients terrified about the prospects of dying . . . and living? In this final chapter we are going to be faced with a scientific challenge: dealing with more "fuzzy," "meaning of life" issues instead of more objective, "hard" data that one can really grab onto, palpate and measure. But such challenges aren't so tangible or simple. The Greek medical terms can describe, but sometimes don't explain. Life is real and so is death: How can we dance close to them, embrace them and understand them? We can take as long as we like to figure out the meaning of life and death, but the clock is ticking. You're preparing to begin a career of taking care of patients, 100% of whom are going to die at some point. Get ready and be ready. Don't look at us for **the** answers. We just teach and write books.

Dr. Elizabeth Kubler-Ross, a pioneering psychiatrist in the area of death and dying, in her work with the terminally ill proposes a clinical model generally descriptive of the dying process. Her five stages are designed as guides, not commandments from Mt. Sinai, in our understanding of what many patients experience on their way to death's door:

1) **Denial**- "Grim Reaper, you must want the party next door. Certainly not me!"
2) **Anger**- "Why me? I've worked hard, paid my taxes, and did what Sister Mary Mary told me to do. It's so damn unfair!"
3) **Bargaining**- "Let's talk. Can't we revise this dying contract a little? God, if you let me do this, then I'll . . . "
4) **Depression**- "Oh, God! Why have you forsaken me! I'm lost!"
5) **Acceptance**- "I'm ready to go."

There are approximately 120 variations of these themes and orders for these themes (just kidding, but at least this is a tangible **number** for those of us who need one).

And with the passing of our patient, there remains the family . . . mourning and living on. What of their grief? They need you, too. Consider some of the common **misconceptions of mourning** the loss of a loved one:

1) "This should be over in a few days." Nope. Stopwatches are not useful in tracking grief. Allow your patients to use their own timetable for emotional healing.
2) "Push those thoughts out of your mind and stay busy!" To the contrary, this is a time to let personal feelings "flow through you" without putting up conditions or barriers. It's not a good time for a lot of changes and planning. Be still. Dealing with a death takes enough energy without coming up with more demands. Sensible exercise, not an Olympian training regime, is indicated.
3) "Don't disturb their privacy." Although licking one's own emotional wounds has its place, the love of dear friends and family helps heal the hollowness of loss. Recall in the Stress Chapter how social support is a major player in stress management, and death is stress!
4) "Grieving is women's work!" Thank goodness that the 1990's have gone a long way in dispelling the notion that "big boys don't cry," particularly when a loved one's loss has rocked one to the core. We all are vulnerable to broken hearts.
5) "Bury the memories and move on." Whoa! Life's most precious possessions are relationships—relationships which transcend death and which deserve honor and respect. It's typically our fear of being left alone that snags the grieving process, not our enduring memories that can continue to serve us well.

If the preceding misconceptions are off the mark, what factors might prove helpful in facilitating the grieving process? Think about these:

1) A support system with heart to heal our loss
2) Adequate sleep and rest
3) Healthy diet
4) Sensible exercise

Not impressed? Hey, it's sometimes the simple stuff that gets the job done! With this biological and personal bedrock, the grieving party can begin to accept what this loss means, feel the heartache, begin living each day without the loved one's presence, and beginning to withdraw the emotional energy entrusted to the deceased and reinvest it in other relationships.

Some barriers may be encountered along the grieving process. Mourners can be tempted to "shut off the pain" through suicidal thoughts and fantasies. Their physical needs may be ignored (i.e., diet, exercise, sleep and rest, and social nourishment). They may become high centered in some stage of the grieving process and become mired down in clinical depression or disruptive anxiety, which they may be tempted to "self-medicate" with alcohol or chemicals. Keep in touch with your mourning patients, if only with a brief but compassionate call or card.

You can tell mourning folks are on the mend when they begin to take care of themselves and their personal needs. They begin to return to the process of living, tuning more into the daily details of getting through the day, sometimes with a smile and lighter heart. They begin to reach out to others beyond just their immediate hurt, moving toward more balanced and "give and take" relationships that involve giving as well as getting. They grow tired of hurting and begin listening to the lighter melodies of life. Finally, they begin to understand that there are at least two kinds of people: those who have danced with the dragons of death and have survived . . . and those who don't even know that such creatures exist.

SUMMARY AND KEY CONCEPTS

As physicians and healers, you need to know a great deal about dying and death. Such wisdom is not contained in a catechism of truth. You need to dig for it . . . in literature, in spiritual tomes, in the words and works of healers, and in modern biomedicine.

This fertile soil has been toiled by the likes of Kubler-Ross, who identifies five **stages of the dying process:**

1) Denial
2) Anger
3) Bargaining
4) Depression
5) Acceptance

Misconceptions of the mourning process present barriers to resolving the dying and death of a loved one. Factors which **facilitate the grieving process** include:

1) Compassionate support system
2) Adequate sleep and rest
3) Healthy diet
4) Exercise

Other writers, researchers, and doctors, like Dr. Kubler-Ross, have marked the journey of the family left behind, the mourners, who have cried the tears of loss and grief . . . and have come to learn the meaning of dying and death. For those who have lost their way along the journey of dying, there will be you—a healer providing a haven from the hell of heartbreak and loss. In the first chapter of this book, we spoke of Fay and her death made easier by a physician who dared to care. Perhaps her story speaks to you: Dare to drink deeply from life . . . and you'll be up to the task.

INDEX

heterocyclic antidepressants, 61
hypersomnia, 86

id, 22
identification, 23
identity vs. role confusion, 115
industry vs. inferiority, 109
infancy, 103
initiative vs. guilt, 109
insomnia, 85
intellectualization, 23
intimacy vs. isolation, 118

Klein-Levin syndrome, 87

latency period, 109
learning handicaps, 111
learning/operant model, 53
lithium, 61
Loeser model of pain levels, 53

marijuana, 79
middle age, 123
midlife crisis, 126
mind/body dualism, 9
modeling, 18
monoamine oxidase inhibitors, 61
Moro's reflex, 105

narcolepsy, 86
narcotics, 79
night terrors, 87
NREM sleep, 84

object constancy, 106
Oedipus conflict, 22
Oedipus/Electra complex, 109
old age, 129
operant conditioning, 14

pain, acute, 52
pain, chronic, 51, 52
palmar grasp reflex, 105
pavor nocturnus, 87
phallic stage, 109
phencyclidine (PCP), 79

postpartum depression, 104
preconscious, 22
Premack principle, 18
presbyopia, 123
projection, 23
psychedelics, 79

reaction formation, 23
Reciprocal Inhibition, Principle of, 48
reductionism, 9
regression, 23
reinforcement, 14, 17
relaxation training, 47
REM sleep, 84
repression, 23
response cost, 16

sedative-hypnotics, 79
Selye, Hans, 43
sexual abuse, 95
shaping, 18
sleep attacks, 86
sleep disorders, 83
sleep paralysis, 87
somnambulism, 87
stimulants, 78
stimulus-response model, 21
stranger anxiety, 105
stress, 43
sublimation, 23
sucking reflex, 105
suicide, 63, 131
superego, 23
suppression, 23
systematic desensitization, 14

therapeutic relationship, 29
time out, 16
token economy, 18
transactional communication,
  29, 31

unconditioned response, 13
unconditioned stimulus, 13
unconscious, 22
undoing, 23